AT THE FOUNTAIN OF ELIJAH

The Carmelite Tradition

WILFRID McGREAL O. Carm

SERIES EDITOR:
Philip Sheldrake

D1388402

DARTON · LONGMAN + TODD

First published in 1999 by
Darton, Longman and Todd Ltd
1 Spencer Court
140–142 Wandsworth High Street
London SW18 4JJ

ISBN 0–232–52265–0

A catalogue record for this book is available from the British Library.

Thanks are due to the following publishers for permission to quote copyright
material: ICS Publications for *The Collected Works of St Teresa of Avila
Volumes 1–3; The Collected Works of St John of the Cross; On the Practice of
the Presence of God; St Thérèse of Lisieux Her Last Conversations; Story of a
Soul; The Poetry of St Thérèse of Lisieux*. Faber and Faber Ltd for 'Choruses
from "The Rock"' by T. S. Eliot, taken from *Collected Poems 1909–62*.

Phototypeset by Intype London Ltd
Printed and bound in Great Britain by
Redwood Books, Trowbridge, Wiltshire

AT THE FOUNTAIN OF ELIJAH

CONTENTS

PREFACE TO THE SERIES

Nowadays, in the Western world, there is a widespread hunger for spirituality in all its forms. This is not confined to traditional religious people let alone to regular churchgoers. The desire for resources to sustain the spiritual quest has led many people to seek wisdom in unfamiliar places. Some have turned to cultures other than their own. The fascination with Native American or Aboriginal Australian spiritualities is a case in point. Other people have been attracted by the religions of India and Tibet or the Jewish Kabbalah and Sufi mysticism. One problem is that, in comparison to other religions, Christianity is not always associated in people's minds with 'spirituality'. The exceptions are a few figures from the past who have achieved almost cult status such as Hildegard of Bingen or Meister Eckhart. This is a great pity for Christianity East and West over two thousand years has given birth to an immense range of spiritual wisdom. Many traditions continue to be active today. Others that were forgotten are being rediscovered and reinterpreted.

It is a long time since an extended series of introductions to Christian spiritual traditions has been available in English. Given the present climate, it is an opportune moment for a new series which will help more people to be aware of the great spiritual riches available within the Christian tradition.

The overall purpose of the series is to make selected spiritual traditions available to a contemporary readership. The books seek to provide accurate and balanced historical and thematic treatments of their subjects. The authors are also conscious of the need to make connections with contemporary experience and values without being artificial or reducing a tradition to one dimension. The authors are well-versed in reliable scholarship about the traditions they describe. However, their intention is that the books should be fresh in style and accessible to the general reader.

One problem that such a series inevitably faces is the word 'spirituality'. For example, it is increasingly used beyond religious circles and does not necessarily imply a faith tradition. Again, it could mean substantially different things for a Christian and a Buddhist. Within Christianity itself, the word in its modern sense is relatively recent. The reality that it stands for differs subtly in the different contexts of time and place. Historically, 'spirituality' covers a breadth of human experience and a wide range of values and practices.

No single definition of 'spirituality' has been imposed on the authors in this series. Yet, despite the breadth of the series there is a sense of a common core in the writers themselves and in the traditions they describe. All Christian spiritual traditions have their source in three things. First, while drawing on ordinary experience and even religious insights from elsewhere, Christian spiritualities are rooted in the scriptures and particularly in the gospels. Second, spiritual traditions are not derived from abstract theory but from attempts to live out gospel values in a positive yet critical way within specific historical and cultural contexts. Third, the experiences and insights of individuals and groups are not isolated but are related to the wider Christian tradition of beliefs, practices and community life. From a Christian perspective, spirituality is not just concerned with prayer or even with narrowly religious activities. It concerns the whole of human life, viewed in terms of a conscious relationship with God, in Jesus Christ, through the indwelling of the Holy Spirit and within a community of believers.

The series as a whole includes traditions that probably would not have appeared twenty years ago. The authors themselves have been encouraged to challenge, where appropriate, inaccurate assumptions about their particular tradition. While conscious of their own biases, authors have nonetheless sought to correct the imbalances of the past. Previous understandings of what is mainstream or 'orthodox' sometimes need to be questioned. People or practices that became marginal demand to be re-examined. Studies of spirituality in the past frequently underestimated or ignored the role of women. Sometimes the treatments of spiritual traditions were culturally one-sided because they were written from an uncritical Western European or North Atlantic perspective.

However, any series is necessarily selective. It cannot hope to do full justice to the extraordinary variety of Christian spiritual traditions. The principles of selection are inevitably open to question. I hope that an appropriate balance has been maintained between a sense of the likely readership on the one hand and the dangers of narrowness on the other. In the end, choices had to be made and the result is inevitably weighted in favour of traditions that have achieved 'classic' status or which seems to capture the contemporary imagination. Within these limits, I trust that the series will offer a reasonably balanced account of what the Christian spiritual tradition has to offer.

As editor of the series I would like to thank all the authors who agreed to contribute and for the stimulating conversations and correspondence that sometimes resulted. I am especially grateful for the high quality of their work which made my task so much easier. Editing such a series is a complex undertaking. I have worked closely throughout with Morag Reeve of Darton, Longman & Todd and Robert Ellsberg of Orbis Books. I am immensely grateful to them for their friendly support and judicious advice. Without them this series would never have come together.

Philip Sheldrake
Sarum College, Salisbury

FOREWORD

In the last fifty years an immense amount of research has been undertaken in the field of Carmelite history and spirituality. I was fortunate as a student in Rome in the 1960s to be able to benefit from Joachim Smet O. Carm, who has done so much for Carmelite historical research, and Otger Steggink O. Carm, who opened up new horizons in my understanding of the Spanish mystics. Alongside these personal contacts a debt of gratitude is owed to Washington Province of the Discalced Carmelites who have produced such fine critical editions of the works of Teresa and John of the Cross. Their ICS publications have also made available critical editions and new translations of the works of Lawrence of the Resurrection, Thérèse of Lisieux and Edith Stein. Such resources are invaluable.

I have also been conscious over the last few years that there is an immense thirst for spirituality. In work with people of all ages and backgrounds and especially with the pilgrims who come to Aylesford I see the need to help people find a living relationship with God – one which will help make sense of the mess that everyday life so often appears to be. I have also been fortunate of late to meet people like Sister Constance Fitzgerald ODC and John Welch O. Carm, both of whom are insightful exponents of the Carmelite tradition of spirituality. Talking to John and Constance has given me the impetus to write. I would also like to thank Chris O'Donnell O. Carm and Paul Chandler O. Carm for their willingness to let me have access to and use some of their work which is as yet unpublished. The Community at Aylesford have given me patient support, Mairin has encouraged me, and Pennie Burton has made sense of my handwriting.

Aylesford
January 1999

INTRODUCTION

Imagination is a key word if we want to explore Carmelite spirituality. Perhaps it would be better to talk about the Carmelite story, because the word 'story' speaks of a living community that is conscious of having good things to share with whoever is willing to take the time to listen and ponder. The Carmelite story is about a journey which in the beginning was from Western Europe to the Holy Land. Over the years, however, journeying to the East has gathered a new meaning. This is not any type of journey, but a pilgrimage. Pilgrimage is an essential part of all religious experience – it is travelling in time and space, but it is also a journey of inner discovery. Carmelites found the goal of their journey in a place and in a person – the mountain that is Carmel and Jesus Christ, to whom they owe total allegiance.

The mountain represents the space and the solitude where the mind and heart can be prepared to listen and pray. It was on that mountain that the first Carmelites gathered, a mountain rich in biblical associations and in its stark beauty an image of God's abundance. The mountain is also linked to the desert and that challenging space has been an image that haunts Carmelites. The desert possesses a majesty and also a mystery – it is a place where we travel, but also a place where we are challenged and purified. Sometimes the journey in the desert can seem long and the absence of familiar signs and consolations can produce a feeling akin to loss. Today in the city, in the turbulence of technological upheaval, we need the desert and we need the mountain. I know that in my own life mountains have meant a great deal. I think of the effort involved in climbing and the discipline and training that is so necessary. The scale of mountains can be inspiring. They can also be dangerous places, subject to sudden change. However, once the peak is reached there is relief, peace and a great sense of the closeness of God. The light and the stillness at 4,000 metres plus is an experience that challenges description. A friend who is a guide in the Alps said you cannot help but pray when you reach a mountain peak.

The Carmelite story also includes two figures from the story of salvation who are powerful symbols for Carmelites, Elijah and Mary. The medieval Carmelites, in creating a myth about their origins, took Mary and Elijah into their story in a special way. Both Elijah and Mary point the way to a special union with God. For Carmelites the insight grew ever clearer that we are called to intimacy with God, tasting of God's presence even in this life, and that this reality is possible for all Christians. If we travel in our minds and hearts we will come to that union. Down the centuries Carmelites have tried to live this out, and the outstanding figures in the Carmelite family have expressed the mystical way for their own generations. The first Carmelites were men, but the tradition expanded to include women in the fifteenth century. Since then their giftedness has enriched the Order. Today the tradition is ready to share its story with a new age, a new culture. The challenge is to keep the original imagination vital and sensitive to the times. Can the story be told and lived as a way for the future? I believe it can and will. There are new possibilities and the journey to the East is evermore open.

There is a tendency to limit an understanding of the Carmelite story to the lives and times of Teresa and John of the Cross. St Teresa of Avila and St John of the Cross are key figures in any study of Carmelite spirituality. These sixteenth-century Spanish mystics are great teachers who share wonderful insights and have helped generations of Christians grow in their relationship with God. However, if we want a way into Carmelite spirituality and if we want to ask what it has to say to people on the threshold of a new millennium, we need to go back to the origins of the Carmelite family. We also need to ask how the original vision has been sustained for some eight hundred years. Above all we need to discover the dynamic of that vision and see how it has been re-imagined in different eras and in different cultures.

The last fifty years have seen a growth in serious study of the origins of the Carmelite Order and the present century has been a time of renewal and growth within the Carmelite family. Paradoxically the upheavals of the twentieth century have strengthened Carmel. The heroic witness of those who opposed the excesses of fascism and the Soviet system has awakened the prophetic sense in the Order. Vatican II with its call for renewal has given a powerful focus in the Order's return to its sources. This has meant a deeper awareness of the earliest days of the Order, the giving of the Rule, its approval and a deeper sense of the symbolic realities that lie at the heart of Carmel.

A contemporary American Carmelite expresses a sense of the Carmelite tradition as it speaks to people today:

> The Carmelite tradition speaks to those who long to be apart, to separate from a smothering existence. The tradition offers the lure of wilderness, mountain retreat, vast expanses of desert. In solitude, in a place apart, we searchers hope to hear our heart's desires more clearly, to reassess life, to dream, to be nourished by hidden springs, to meet the One whom others speak of with great assurance. Those who are drawn by the Carmelite tradition are often pilgrims to places unknown, trusting the testimony of others who have taken the same ancient path.[1]

I would like to unravel the story of the Carmelite tradition and to do so it will be necessary to travel down the centuries and see the tradition growing and flourishing in many amazing ways.

The earliest Carmelites were pilgrims and hermits who settled on Mount Carmel at the end of the twelfth century. They were poor men seeking to follow Jesus Christ. They lived on a mountain that was rich in history and symbolism. It had been the home of Elijah the Prophet, it was seen as a symbol of God's abundance, an image of beauty and of the generosity of God's grace. It was also a place apart, an oasis in the desert, a place of living waters where the seeker after God could drink from the well of life. The Carmelites were not to find a permanent home on Mount Carmel as the politics of that time caused them to be scattered throughout the known world, but they would always carry this memory with them as a creative source that would constantly help to renew the Carmelite tradition.

When the Carmelites came to Europe around 1240 they encountered hostility and misunderstanding. However, their way of life was approved by Pope Innocent IV and they began to live their contemplative life in the towns. They wanted to preserve the spirit of solitude and yet they were willing to bring the Gospel to the people. Being poor, dependent on alms, the Carmelites were gradually inserted into the mendicant move-ment. The tensions of living the Rule led to modifications in the fifteenth century, yet the basic spirit remained as evidenced in works like *The Book of the First Monks*. John Soreth, a fifteenth-century Prior General, was a vigorous reformer, and other groups challenged those who would acquiesce with the spirit of the times. In fact, the fifteenth century saw the emerg-ence of the first convents of Carmelite nuns in France and the Low Countries.

The Reformation dealt severe blows to Carmel in Northern Europe, but John Rossi who became General at the end of the Council of Trent in 1564 undertook a programme of reform from within. He listened to a Spanish Carmelite nun, Teresa – the great Teresa of Avila – and endorsed her vision of returning to the Rule of 1247. He also gave a cautious welcome to the reform of the friars whose genius was to be John of the Cross. Teresa and John are pivotal figures in the story of Carmel, creative and imaginative personalities who rank as great mystics. Their reforming work has affected not just Carmel, but the Church at large. Sadly the reform occasioned misunderstanding that led to division in the Order, a division that is only finding healing at the end of the twentieth century.

The creative energy that flowed from John and Teresa was to have a profound effect on the whole Carmelite family. In seventeenth-century France the writings and the presence of John of St Samson and Lawrence of the Resurrection, neither of whom had a formal theological background, continued the work of renewal with their overwhelming consciousness of God's gift of love. These two men were to be powerful influences in the formation of many young friars in their native France.

The last hundred years have seen a number of remarkable Carmelite men and women who have transcended the spirit of their age to make the tradition of Carmel live in the popular imagination. Thérèse of Lisieux and Elizabeth of Dijon were both mystics who during their short lives produced a body of teaching rooted in Scripture that is both profound and simple. Thérèse was able to get to the heart of Paul's teaching on the mystical body and live it as 'love at the heart of the Church'. Elizabeth in her turn expressed the doctrine of the Trinity with a simplicity that drew people to the mystery, giving them a way into the reality of the community of love that is the Godhead. Elizabeth and Thérèse restore the link between spirituality and theology that gives them an added importance. However, the focus in this study will be on Thérèse rather than Elizabeth of Dijon.

The twentieth century has seen immense technological progress, but also assaults on the human being on a scale never equalled in history. Ideologies pursued relentlessly have destroyed thousands of lives and even with the demise of Communism the human agenda is still dominated by forms of materialism. The human spirit, the fullness of life, has become a casualty of the twentieth century.

It is in this context that we must look at figures like Titus Brandsma and Edith Stein. Both Titus and Edith died in Nazi concentration camps. Titus went there because of his opposition to racism and Edith because she was born Jewish. They were both deeply contemplative and also searching intellects.

They were of one mind in rooting themselves in Carmelite tradition, making the mystics come alive for their contemporaries. Titus used his gifts as a communicator in a prophetic way by attacking Nazi ideology and supporting fellow Christians. Edith, who wrote of the science of the Cross, suffered because of her race and died like Christ at the hands of the unjust.

Since Vatican II, the Carmelite tradition has recognised the growing thirst for spirituality. Carmelites working in the developing world have realised that the option for the poor challenges them to live in the prophetic spirit of Elijah. Elijah has always been one of the great symbolic figures of Carmel and as a prophet he both had a thirst for justice and kept alive a generous memory that challenged the status quo.

Issues of justice have moulded late twentieth-century spirituality and one that affects Christianity and asks questions of any tradition of spirituality is our attitude to women. Many great figures of Carmel have been women, and Mary along with Elijah is a great symbolic figure. How can she help the Carmelite way to be creative in speaking to both men and women? We need a spirituality with substance and we need ways that are inclusive, so the challenge to the Carmelite tradition must be to speak imaginatively and purposefully to all peoples.

Any attempt to understand the Carmelite tradition does demand then a journey in time and space. It means going back to the last decades of the twelfth century and entering a world of intense commitment and new found vitality. It was an era of charismatic figures in all walks of life and a time when ordinary people were finding greater freedom to express their spiritual aspirations. This is the moment when the Carmelite tradition comes into being.

1. THE FIRST HERMITS – A WAY OF LIFE

The first Carmelites have left very little in the way of historical and biographical detail. They were part of a movement in the second half of the twelfth century that was to have a profound impact on the life of the Church. Twelfth-century Europe was a time of growth fostered by greater political stability and economic development. It was the time of the Crusades, of growing wealth, of travel and a period of intellectual stirrings. It was also a time of reaction in the Church, including a search for a way of living Christianity that was closer to the Gospel. The power of the institutional Church was growing, but an effective pastoral presence was often lacking. Movements of 'poor' people who sought Christ emerged, and one of these groups was to become the Franciscan way. Others saw the great pilgrimage to the Holy Land as a way to follow Christ in a literal, historical sense. They wanted to journey to the Holy Land and be in the very places where Jesus had announced the Kingdom of God and had suffered and died on account of his mission.

The Crusades had opened up the Holy Land and made it possible for Christians from the West to visit the holy places and even to settle. However, the situation was complex and the western presence in the Holy Land was tenuous, dependent on military power and diplomatic compromises. In the twelfth century many pilgrims began to live as hermits in the Holy Land and also made contact with hermits of the Greek tradition. The Saracens, however, began to push the Crusaders towards the sea so that by the last decades of the twelfth century the hermits would have been forced to withdraw to the coastal area near Acre and Sidon. It was about this time, 1190, that some hermits began to organise themselves on Mount Carmel and it is this group that stands at the origins of the Carmelite tradition.

At this point it is helpful to reflect on our understanding of who these hermits were and what they stood for. They were part of the evangelical awakening of the time – people fuelled by a desire to live their lives in close conformity to the Gospel. Such people looked for a way of life that flowed from the Gospel. Christ was the focus of their attention. It was his way of life and that of the Apostles that provided the inspiration. Pilgrimage, poverty, a way of living inspired by the first Christian community in Jerusalem – these were the essential components of this way of life.

Pilgrimage was penitential. In essence it meant radical change, for it marked a break with one's previous relation to society. It meant loosening the bonds of convention and letting go. Going to the Holy Land was seen as enabling a Christian to find a new way of meeting Christ. It was above all an encounter with the humanity of Jesus Christ. Jerusalem, which was the most important goal of this journey, was perceived as the centre of the world and the pivot between the old covenant and the new. Jerusalem was also a symbol of the eternal, it was a place full of eschatological meaning. These pilgrims were in general poor men. They had no pretensions to any rank or status because for them poverty was an essential part of their life. Because they were poor and had no desire for privilege, they were not committed to the use or misuse of power. They realised that the Christian presence in the Holy Land had nothing to do with winning back the holy places by military force. What mattered was a spiritual renewal. They would be there as a presence of people who wanted to live in the spirit of the Gospel.

These are the circumstances that lay behind the emergence of the first hermits on Mount Carmel. They were not organised like a religious order, but came from the poor, the penitents, the pilgrims. They were close to the people, speaking from their hearts. People admired their simplicity, their poverty and the way they tried to live like the first Christians. Such groups could be, and were to some degree, seen as a threat by the clergy. For instance, who gave these hermits the right to preach? What mattered however was that the ordinary folk felt a rapport with the hermits. There was no social division, rather they were brothers speaking to their own. They depended on the people with whom they shared God's word and received in turn the basics of life. These hermits were to become the first mendicants. They lived on the edge of towns near to the people, but they were not taken over or overtaken by society.

The first Carmelites were such hermits, poor men, brothers who shared God's word with the people. They had come to live on Mount Carmel around the last decades of the twelfth century. Mount Carmel is just a few kilometres to the east of Haifa. Looking at Carmel as a boat approaches the coast it is more like an extended ridge than a mountain, rising no more than 2,000 feet above sea level. On the landward side Carmel is scored by small valleys or ravines with springs of water flowing out among the rocks. The first Carmelites settled in one of these sheltered spots near the fountain of Elijah. It is possible that a Byzantine group had established a presence there. Certainly the Wadi Ain-es-Sah was steeped in sacred tradition. This group of hermits on Carmel began to achieve an identity and Jacques de Vitry, who was Bishop of Acre, c.1216 observes: 'Others after the example and in imitation of the holy solitary Elijah, the Prophet, lived as hermits in the beehives of small cells on Mount Carmel . . . near the spring which is called the Spring of Elijah.'[1]

Towards the end of the first decade of the thirteenth century the hermits on Carmel approached Albert, the Latin Patriarch of Jerusalem, to give them a way of life. Albert was elected Patriarch of Jerusalem in 1206. Prior to that he had been Bishop of Bobbio and Vercelli. He came to the Holy Land with over twenty years experience as a bishop, a man of integrity and discernment. He had begun life as a Canon Regular of

Mortura, so he understood the project of committing one's life to Jesus Christ and had also gained experience in helping groups of poor men organise themselves into communities.

This group that asked Albert for a way of life had already achieved some sense of community. They had a degree of orga- nisation, including a leader, and now they felt the time had come to codify and give some structure to already existing relationships. Albert used his skills and knowledge of how the Church could respond to such a group with its various needs, and gave a direction and a unity to the hermits on Carmel.

When Albert gave the hermits on Carmel a 'way of life' sometime between 1206 and 1214, he began a process that was to culminate in the approval of the text as a Rule by Pope Innocent IV in 1247 in the Bull *Quem honorem Conditoris*. By his intervention Albert gave a way of life to a group of lay people living in common. He was not so much founding a religious order as recognising a community. The hermits were different in so far as they did not follow one of the recognised rules, such as the Rule of St Benedict or that of St Augustine, and in the eyes of some people they were considered as lay men. However, in 1229 Gregory IX confirmed their way of life and called it a Rule and at the same time prohibited the possession of property outside their hermitage. This approach was perhaps influenced by the Pope's dealings with Fran- ciscans.

However, because the fear of persecution drove a large group of hermits to the West from 1238 onward, the potential for change arose. This surfaced in the General Chapter of 1247 held at Aylesford (a meeting of Carmelites from all over Europe and the Holy Land), when delegates were sent to Innocent IV with the request that Carmelites could be permitted to pass 'to a state where they could have the joy of being useful to themselves and others'.

The response to this request was the papal document *Quem honorem Conditoris*, which 'proclaimed, corrected and miti- gated The Rule'. The pronouncement removed any doubt about the status of the brothers and added to the promise of obedience the need to observe chastity and renounce property. This gave Albert's form of life the same status as the Franciscan Rule (approved in 1223).

The form of life given by Albert along with Innocent IV's additions is a concise document. What follows is a modern translation. The earliest text is in normal type and additions made when the Rule was approved in 1247 are noted in italics. The division into chapters is a late addition and was introduced by the Prior General, Giovanni Battista Caffardi, in 1586. These headings are therefore placed in brackets.

[Introduction:]
Albert, called by God's favour to be Patriarch of the church of Jerusalem, bids health in the Lord and the blessing of the Holy Spirit to his beloved sons in Christ, B[rocard] and the other hermits under obedience to him, who live near the spring on Mount Carmel.

Many and varied are the ways in which our saintly forefathers laid down how everyone, whatever his station or the kind of religious observance he has chosen, should live a life of allegiance to Jesus Christ – how, pure in heart and stout in conscience, he must be unswerving in the service of his Master. It is to me, however, that you have come for a rule of life in keeping with your avowed purpose, a rule you may hold fast to henceforward; and therefore:

[Chapter 1]
The first thing I require of you is to have a prior, one of yourselves, who is to be chosen for the office by common consent, or that of the greater or maturer part of you. Each of the others must provide him obedience – of which, once promised, he must try to make his deeds the true reflection *and also chastity and the renunciation of ownership.*

[Chapter 2]
If the prior and the brothers see fit, you may have foun-

dations in solitary places, or where you are given a site that is suitable and convenient for the observance proper to your Order.

[Chapter 3]
Next, each one of you is to have a separate cell, situated as the lie of the land you propose to occupy may dictate, and allotted by disposition of the prior with agreement of the other brothers, or the more mature among them.

[Chapter 4]
However, you are to eat whatever may have been given you in a common refectory, listening together meanwhile to a reading from Holy Scripture where that can be done without difficulty.

[Chapter 5]
None of the brothers is to occupy a cell other than that allotted to him or to exchange cells with one another, without leave of whoever is prior at the time.

[Chapter 6]
The prior's cell should stand near the entrance to your property, so that he may be the first to meet those who approach, and whatever has to be done in consequence may all be carried out as he may decide and order.

[Chapter 7]
Each one of you is to stay in his cell or nearby, pondering the Lord's law day and night and keeping watch at his prayers unless attending to some other duty.

[Chapter 8]
Those who know how to say the canonical hours with those in orders should do so, in the way those holy forefathers of ours laid down, and according to the church's approved custom. Those who do not know the hours must say twenty-five Our Fathers for the night office, except on Sundays and solemnities when that number is to be doubled so that Our Father is said fifty times; the same prayer must

be said seven times in the morning place of Lauds, and seven times too for each of the other hours, except for Vespers when it must be said fifteen times.

[Chapter 9]
None of the brothers is to lay claim to anything as his own, but you are to possess everything in common; and from those things that the Lord will give you, each is to receive from the prior – that is the brother he appoints for the purpose – whatever befits his age and needs. You may have as many asses and mules as you need, however, and may keep a certain amount of livestock or poultry.

[Chapter 10]
An oratory should be built as conveniently as possible among the cells, where, if it can be done without difficulty, you are to gather each morning to hear Mass.

[Chapter 11]
On Sundays too, or other days if necessary, you should discuss matters of discipline and your spiritual welfare; and on this occasion indiscretions and failings of the brothers, if any be found at fault, should be lovingly corrected.

[Chapter 12]
You are to fast every day, except Sundays, from the feast of the Exaltation of the Holy Cross until Easter Day, unless bodily sickness or feebleness, or some other good reason, demand a dispensation for the fast; for necessity overrides every law.

[Chapter 13]
You are to abstain from meat, except as a remedy for sickness or feebleness. But as, when you are on a journey, you more often than not have to beg your way; outside your own houses you may eat foodstuffs that have been cooked with meat, so as to avoid giving trouble to your hosts. At sea, meat may be eaten.

[Chapter 14]

Since man's life on earth is a time of trial, and all who live devotedly to Christ must undergo persecution, and the devil your foe is on the prowl like a roaring lion looking for prey to devour, you must use every care to clothe yourselves in God's armour so that you may be ready to withstand the enemy's ambush. Your loins are to be girt with chastity, your breast fortified by holy meditations, for, as Scripture has it, holy meditation will save you. Put on holiness as your breastplate, and it will enable you to love the Lord your God with all your heart and soul and strength, and your neighbour as yourself. Faith must be your shield on all occasions, and with it you will be able to quench all the flaming missiles of the wicked one; there can be no pleasing God without faith; and the victory lies in this – your faith. On your head set the helmet of salvation, and so be sure of deliverance by our only Saviour, who sets his own free from their sins. The sword of the spirit, the word of God, must abound in your mouths and hearts. Let all you do have the Lord's word for accompaniment.

[Chapter 15]

You must give yourselves to work of some kind, so that the devil may always find you busy; no idleness on your part must give him a chance to pierce the defences of your souls. In this respect you have both the teaching and the example of St Paul the Apostle, into whose mouth Christ put his own words. God made him preacher and teacher of faith and truth to the nations: with him as your leader you cannot go astray. We live among you, he said, labouring and weary, toiling night and day so as not to be a burden to any of you; not because we had no power to do otherwise but so as to give you, in your own selves, an example you might imitate. For the charge we gave you when we were with you was this: that whoever is not willing to work should not be allowed to eat either. For we have heard that there are certain restless idlers among you. We charge people of this kind, and implore them in the name of our Lord Jesus Christ, that they earn their own bread by silent toil. This is the way of holiness and goodness: see that you follow it.

[Chapter 16]
The Apostle would have us keep silence, for in silence he tells us to work. As the prophet also makes known to us: Silence is the way to foster holiness. Elsewhere he says: Your strength will lie in silence and hope. For this reason I lay down that you are to keep silence from after Compline until after Prime the next day. At other times, although you need not keep silence so strictly, be careful not to indulge in a great deal of talk, for, as Scripture has it – and experience teaches us no less – sin will not be wanting where there is much talk, and he who is careless in speech will come to harm; and elsewhere: The use of many words brings harm to the speaker's soul. And Our Lord says in the gospel: Every rash word uttered will have to be accounted for on judgement day. Make a balance then, each of you, to weigh his words in; keep a tight rein on your mouths, lest you should stumble and fall in speech, and your fall be irreparable and prove mortal. Like the Prophet, watch your step lest your tongue give offence, and employ every care in keeping silent, which is the way to foster holiness.

[Chapter 17]
You, Brother Brocard, and whoever may succeed you as prior, must always keep in mind and put into practice what our Lord said in the gospel: Whoever has a mind to become a leader among you must make himself servant to the rest, and whichever of you would be the first must become your bondsman.

[Chapter 18]
You other brothers too, hold your prior in humble rever-

ence, your minds not on him but on Christ who has placed him over you, and who, to those who rule the churches, addressed the words: Whoever pays you heed pays heed to me, and whoever treats you with dishonour dishonours me; if you remain so minded you will not be found guilty of contempt, but will merit life eternal as fit reward for your obedience.

Here then are a few points I have written down to provide you with a standard of conduct to live up to; but our Lord, at his second coming, will reward anyone who does more than he is obliged to do. See that the bounds of common sense are not exceeded, however, for common sense is the guide of the virtues.[2]

During the remaining years of the thirteenth century, confirmations of Innocent's Bull followed and, by the end of the century, Boniface VIII had removed any doubts about the status of the Carmelites as a group of religious.

Short as the Carmelite Rule is, it is rich in meaning and crucial for any understanding of Carmelite spirituality. There are over seventy commentaries on the Rule, many from the medieval period and some that are contemporary. The Rule that the whole Carmelite family observes is that of 1247, Innocent IV's approved text. It is the document that enabled the hermits of Carmel to live in Europe and become part of the mendicant movement. As Joachim Smet observes, 'The Carmelite Rule of 1247 brought solitude to the town when life in the desert was no longer feasible ... and all reforms in Carmel have always been to their contemplative origins.'[3]

What is at the heart of the Carmelite Rule and how can it speak to us today? What does it have to say to people at large?

The essence of the Rule is the desire to live a life of allegiance to Jesus Christ, serving him faithfully with a pure heart and a clear conscience. These words that echo St Paul are crucial to an understanding of the Carmelite way. As the Constitutions of the Order state, Carmelites live their life of allegiance to Christ through a commitment to seek the face of the living

God through community and through service in the midst of the people.

The notion of allegiance to Christ had a special meaning for the first Carmelites. They saw their allegiance in some degree as that of loyal vassals to their master. They were part of a struggle on behalf of Christ to free the Holy Land from the Saracens, yet they realised that an armed struggle was not the way, as the Holy Land, and indeed the world, would only be won for Christ if people fought for spiritual values. Jesus Christ claimed their total allegiance as they strove to work for the deepest living of the Gospel and all the values that Jesus represented. This is why in later chapters the Rule speaks of a spiritual struggle which needs the shield of faith and other strategies to outflank the forces of darkness. The images and language are those of St Paul, and the sense of personal struggle by the early Carmelites echoes desert spirituality. In that warfare spiritual arms are needed. However, this struggle has moved from the warfare of the Crusaders, who fought an external enemy, to the deeper struggle where light and truth face up to the powers of darkness. The vision is of John's Gospel where the light will not be overcome by the dark and truth is the source of freedom. Carmel is a space for growth and a place of struggle. Carmel was the scene for the great contest between Elijah and the priests of Baal where God was vindicated. This sets a special seal on the place for all time (1 Kings 18).

To live in allegiance to Christ in loving obedience is the hallmark of all Christians. Christ on the Cross saves us through his loving obedience and our following of Christ is meant to reproduce that commitment of love. The faithfulness to Christ is enhanced for a Carmelite by a love of his law – his word. The Rule is shot through with scriptural quotations and allusions. Reflecting on the word of God is central to the project. Carmelites knew the law of God because they listened to God's word through meditation, solitude and watchful prayer. The concrete living out of all this is achieved by obeying the Prior. In obeying the Prior they saw themselves as obeying one placed over them by Christ. However, the Prior was to exercise his authority as Christ would have done – as a servant. 'Whoever wants to be first among you, let him be your servant.' This vision of the leader of the community sees him as very different from the Benedictine abbot. The Prior is the servant, not the father of the community. The relationship is not one of mutual obedience between father and sons but rather an attitude of faithfulness inspired by the common goal of a faithful following of Christ.

The working out of the relationship between the Prior and the rest of the community is important. The formula for living looks towards an interchange of ideas and aspirations. The brothers are to meet to discuss matters of importance, so that the common life and the well-being of each brother is discussed. The Prior then executes what has been decided. He is also the one who welcomes visitors and ensures that hospitality and the needs of the community are not in conflict. Issues like where the brothers should make foundations are also part of this community discernment, along with the allocation of separate cells for each brother. However, once decisions are made, the Prior has the task of ensuring that any changes are made at his behest. The picture that emerges is very much of a community project where the Prior is entrusted with the oversight of the community's decision. He becomes to a degree the conscience or ongoing memory of the community.

The Prior is, therefore, not there to exert power or to achieve status. He is meant to be a person who serves the community. If the Prior really imitates Christ as the Servant of the Lord, he becomes a symbol of the community's faithfulness to God through Jesus Christ. The whole structure of the community and the relationships that exist inside that community need to be always and ever more Christocentric. One other element that is in the Rule, and perhaps sometimes neglected, is the fact that there is no distinction between those who are ordained and the laity. Except in so far as a priest is presumed for daily Eucharist, priesthood is not taken into account. The only distinction that is made is between those who can read and those who cannot. Those who can read must pray the Canonical Hours.

In any attempt to understand or live the Rule there can be conflict between its eremitical aspect and the community dimension. Such interpretations can be culturally conditioned or come through a particular focus. Again it is often easier to posit an opposition than to work towards a creative unity which will often have its own tensions.

Some commentators have taken Chapter 7 to be the heart of the Rule: 'Each one of you is to stay in his own cell or nearby, pondering the Lord's Law day and night and keeping watch in prayer unless attending to some other duty.' This envisages an engagement of the mind and heart where a brother is so absorbed by the Scriptures that God's word is in his heart and mind at all times. The solitude and silence that surrounds the Carmelite enables the focus to be on God and God's word. However, even from the earliest days of the Carmelite project, the brothers left their solitude to preach and share their love of God's word with people. From 1247 onwards they had opted for the mendicant life, which in principle meant mobility and association with the growing urban culture of Western Europe. In the context of a commitment to the apostolate as well as eremitical life, meditation came to mean an ever deepening reflection on the Scriptures, so that people at large could be helped by their insight and preaching. The brother is also expected to be vigilant in prayer so that he is ready to welcome the Lord when he comes again. A consequence of this vigilance is a growth in sensitivity in being aware that we must not allow our hearts to grow coarse or lessen the ardour of our love for our neighbour. Later chapters of the Rule with their focus on spiritual warfare and commitment to fraternal living give a more focused realisation of the call to vigilant prayer.

However, the overall tenor of this chapter is to praise and value the solitude that enables prayer, not in the sense of a flight from life, but rather to gain the energy, focus and vitality

to work with people and above all to practise love as brothers
in community at the service of other people.

Given these considerations, modern commentators on the
Rule have suggested that the heart of the Rule is not just
Chapter 7, but Chapters 7–11. The Rule does not just envisage
isolated persons praying in their cells, but rather a community
who journeyed in unity. Here we can feel the inspiration of the
Acts of the Apostles depicting the early Christians in Jerusalem. These chapters take us from solitude to a celebration
of praise as the Psalms are prayed in common. There is a
sharing of goods, an openness to poverty and also a sharing of
ideals and needs in regular meetings. All this culminates in
the celebration of the daily Eucharist. If anything is at the
heart of the Rule it is the daily celebration of the Eucharist
and the brotherly communion that it achieves.

The following of Christ, the great project of the Rule, is
achieved by becoming a community of disciples who owe everything to Christ. Discipleship in a community means that the
Carmelite lives in Christ. It means that the Rule is not
interested in an individualistic spirituality, but rather in the
realisation of ecclesial communion. To reflect on God's word
in solitude energises and leads to community centred on the
Eucharist and then to the living out of that love with one's
brother. The fraternity that grows from this prayer and celebration is not severe or harshly ascetic nor is it over-
enthusiastic. The Rule has no place for penalties, but envisages
the interaction of community meetings and the role of the
Prior as a servant brother as being to achieve a commitment
to keep the ideal of generosity vibrant. Freedom to serve
emerges from this dynamic love and from the encounter with
God that arises from pondering God's word in the heart.

An energy and symbol that is found in the Carmelite Rule
is Jerusalem. The journey to Jerusalem was the original inspiration of the first Carmelites. However, the central chapters of
the Rule are obviously inspired by the vision of the Jerusalem
community found in Acts chapters 2 and 4: a community of
disciples who were fervent in prayer, sharing all in common

and bonded by the breaking of bread. The first Jerusalem community was a community of prayer and a community that attracted others by the quality of its being. The Carmelite Rule is shaped and inspired by that ideal, an ideal that is always being called into being in every generation.

2. CHANGE AND TENSION

The second half of the thirteenth century was a time of growth, transition and tension for Carmelites. However, in understanding the period and the development of the Carmelite tradition of spirituality, it is important that we do not impose agendas from a later period. The Order had to wait until 1326 for Pope John XXII's Bull *Super Cathedram* (issued in 1300) to extend to the Carmelites the same privileges and exemptions that were enjoyed by the Franciscans and Dominicans. That declaration removed any hint of ambiguity about the Order's status and allowed the friars to take on legitimate apostolic work: preaching, teaching, public churches and so on. It also eased relationships with local bishops. During this time the internal government of the Order took shape and scores of foundations were made throughout Europe from Scotland to Spain and eastwards.

However, while foundations were made in towns and the first brothers went to the universities, there were still many in the Order who followed the hermit tradition by living in remote places like Hulne in Northumberland. Carmelites were only finally forced to leave Mount Carmel and the Holy Land in 1291.

There was, therefore, still a deep sense of solitude, silence and the desert. The Rule speaks of spiritual warfare and that struggle goes on in the desert. If the desert is carefully tended it flourishes. By this is meant not so much a physical space, but rather the geography of the heart. Silence and solitude combine to create the conditions where God can be all in all. John Welch expresses this inner beauty and transfiguration:

A desert carefully tended becomes a garden. In the imagination of Carmelites, Mount Carmel represents not only the solitude in which the hermit wrestles demons, but it also represents the flowering of new, verdant life. The invitation to Carmel offered by the tradition is an invitation to open one's life to the loving activity of God and so to the blossoming of one's life. The garden is a counter-symbol to the desert. Mount Carmel represented solitude and stark battle to the Carmelite, but it was also a place of physical beauty which offered fresh water, thick forest, striking vistas, and the company of wild animals.[1]

It is in this context of change and tension that Nicholas the Frenchman appears. He was Prior General from 1266 to 1271. From his writing it is evident that he was a person of some learning, with a familiarity not just with the Scriptures but also with Aristotle and other classical writers. He visited the various provinces of the Order from England to Sicily and was well acquainted with what was afoot. It would seem that he had lived as a hermit and was none too pleased with the movement towards the active life. He wrote a passionate treatise, *The Flaming Arrow*, a moving appeal to the brothers to return to the spirit of the desert.

It seems that his plea found little support, and in 1271 Nicholas resigned his office of Prior General. The treatise is not so much an attack on the apostolic life as a caring criticism of those who would take up the apostolate without preparation and foresight. There was a need for prayerful responsibility and a sense of how exacting the apostolate could be. It was not enough to feel the urge to preach – there was the need to be properly formed: education was a prerequisite. Interestingly, by the next decade Carmelites were taking their place in the universities. Nicholas' strictures against the presumptuous preachers are blunt in the extreme:

They prate away before the common folk – without understanding a word of their own rigmarole – as bold-faced as though theology lay digested in the stomach of their memory, and any tale will serve their turn if it can be given a mystical twist and made to redound to their own glory. Then, when they have done preaching – or rather tale-telling, there they stand, ears all pricked up and itching, to catch the slightest whisper of flattery but not a vestige do they show of the endowments for which, in their appetite for vainglory, they long to be praised.

What is it indeed but a foolish craving for human praise and the vain glory it occasions that moves men like these to preach, devoid as they are of learning and right conduct alike? If they achieve anything at all by their words, they bring it to naught again by their example. The ambitious presumption, the consummate impudence of these unlettered creatures, whose moral conduct deserves nothing but contempt, in trying to usurp the office of preaching, is not only an abuse, it is sheer absurdity.[2]

The Flaming Arrow is not easy reading and the hyperbole can at times seem to be for rhetorical effect and nothing else. However, there are passages of poignant beauty and deep personal revelation. Nicholas' picture of desert life and the blessings it brings could well be based on his memories of life on Carmel. Whatever the inspiration, this is a classic presentation of the blessings of solitude:

In the desert [*in solitudine*] all the elements conspire to favour us. The heavens, resplendent with the stars and planets in their amazing order, bear witness by their beauty to the mysteries higher still. The birds seem to assume the nature of angels, and tenderly console us with their gentle caroling. The mountains too, as Isaiah prophesied, 'drop down sweetness' incomparable upon us, and the friendly hills 'flow with milk and honey' such as is never tasted by the foolish lovers of this world. When we sing the praises of our Creator, the mountains about us, our brother conventuals, resound with corresponding hymns of praise to the Lord, echoing back our voices and filling the air with strains of harmony as though accompanying our song upon stringed instruments. The roots in their growth, the grass in its greenness, the leafy boughs and trees – all make merry in their own ways as they echo our praise and the flowers in their loveliness, as they pour out their delicious fragrance, smile their best for the consolation of us solitaries. The sunbeams, though tongueless, speak saving messages to us. The shady bushes rejoice to give us shelter. In short, every creature we see or hear in the desert gives us friendly refreshment and comfort; indeed, for all their silence they tell forth wonders, and move the interior man to give praise to the creator – so much more wonderful than themselves.[3]

The images and the cumulative power of the passage evoke parallels with the poetry of John of the Cross. Nicholas felt that he had failed the Order and that perhaps he should never have taken the office of Prior General:

Is it not my ardent love for you – excessive perhaps – that has kept my soul in such a state of infatuation that I hardly knew who I was, what I was, where I was, or what I should do?

Out of devoted love for you it was that I sailed the seas and journeyed from country to country, that I spent my time and wore out my body; and all my persistent labour for your good, in the face of opposition from your stepsons, has been in vain, for I have brought you no profit. Apart from the merit of my good intentions, then, I count as lost all the heavenly treasure I could have been laying up all this time in a solitary cell.[4]

In *The Flaming Arrow* Nicholas articulates a problem that will remain at the heart of the Carmelite project: how the vision of the desert and a sense of solitude can combine with apostolic activity. For Nicholas it was not a case that they were incompatible. Rather, there was a need to work out a creative synthesis which would require great discipline on a personal level and great care in the formation of friars. Nicholas felt overwhelmed by the sense of change and could not follow up his diagnosis with any sense of optimism for the future. Coping with change is always a challenge, how we make transitions that are seamless needs sensitivity. Nicholas is important in so far as he reminds us of the danger of superficiality and of losing life-giving memories.

However, the Priors General that followed Nicholas were all men who had a deep attachment to the hermit tradition and were able to guide the Order along its new path. Peter of Millau, who succeeded Ralph Fresburn around 1276, carried out his duties with amazing energy. He was assiduous in visiting communities and enabled the friars to enter the universities to acquire the formation that would help them articulate those things they had learnt in prayer. It was said of him that to talk to him was to learn contemplation. His successor Raymond de L'Ile was cast in a similar mould and after three years in office retired to a life of solitude in 1297. It would seem that those leading figures in the Order were not as aware of contradictions between old and new as Nicholas had been. They lived the truth that authentic activity is the fruit of contemplation.

3. ELIJAH AND MARY – SEARCH FOR IDENTITY

The move to Europe and the rapid expansion of the Order in the second half of the thirteenth century led to a search for identity among the younger Carmelites. What could they say to people about their origins when they were unable to specify a date of foundation or point to a founder like Francis or Dominic? The first recorded attempt to answer the questions about Carmelite origins came in the opening lines of the Constitutions of the Order drawn up at the General Chapter held in London in 1281. This answer is known as the *Rubrica Prima*:

> We declare, bearing testimony to the truth, that from the time when the prophets Elijah and Elisha dwelt devoutly on Mount Carmel, holy Fathers both of the Old and New Testament, whom the contemplation of heavenly things drew to the solitude of the same mountain, have without doubt led praiseworthy lives there by the fountain of Elijah in holy penitence unceasingly and successfully maintained.
>
> It was these same successors whom Albert the patriarch of Jerusalem in the time of Innocent III united into a community, writing a rule for them which Pope Honorius, the successor of the same Innocent, and many of their successors, approving this Order, most devoutly confirmed by their charters. In the profession of this rule, we, their followers, serve the Lord in diverse parts of the world, even to the present day.[1]

As Joachim Smet observes in his history of the Carmelites,

this was the seed from which the tradition about Elijah was
to grow. The Carmelites saw themselves as successors to the
school of prophets that had existed on Carmel and also to a
long tradition in the Christian era of hermits who had chosen
Carmel as their home. The notion that Carmelites were in a
line of descent from Elijah and Elisha was taken at a later
date to involve a literal succession and became the cause of
bitter disputes. The Rubric when first written was intended to
situate the emerging Order in a tradition and also to see Elijah
as an archetype and exemplar. The notion of Elijah as one who
stood before God in prayer and witnessed to God's truth before
the powerful resonated with late thirteenth-century Carmelites as they tried to bridge the hermit and mendicant elements.
Paul Chandler comments on the Order's tradition about Elijah:

> It has always seen him as the first Carmelite and a rich
> model of the Carmelite way of life ... we consider him as
> a man on a journey, always on the way from 'here' to 'there'
> in response to God's call and in this sense we see that
> the Elijah of the Scriptures and the Elijah of Carmelite
> tradition are one. God's grace does not allow him to be
> still. It calls him to grow and become. It was not easy for
> him; his weaknesses and fears had to be overcome. But in
> the care of God's love and in the strength that comes from
> his grace the journey was not too long.[2]

The journey image is powerful – in its essence it is always
about our journey into the core of our being, but it is also the
pilgrimage to the East to Jerusalem or, as with Elijah, to
Cherith when God is experienced.

The Carmelite tradition about Elijah and to a lesser extent
Mary is found in the *Liber de Institutione Primorum Monachorum*. This document in its present form is the work of Felip
Ribot, who was Prior Provincial of the Catalonian Province,
and the probable date of compilation is 1370. The Australian
Carmelite Paul Chandler has done much to make this document accessible to the contemporary reader.

After the Rule it is possibly the key work in any understanding of Carmelite spirituality and certainly from 1400 onwards dominated the Carmelites' historical thinking and their vision of the Order. It contains all the key themes of Carmelite spirituality: allegiance to Christ, openness to Scriptures, the sense of silence and solitude and the undivided heart. Marian elements also emerge, but above all there is an underlying sense of God's presence and protection found in intimate prayer. The work is full of symbols: the mountain, the desert, the brook Cherith and the little cloud that prefigures Mary.

The work is a synthesis of older Carmelite traditions and the way Carmelites of that period read Scripture. What is crucial is the way it came to colour Carmelite thinking about the very essence of the Order and, above all, it is the expression of the Elijan tradition.

Paul Chandler raises an issue about the work that helps our understanding in a most positive way. He sees in these writings the early Carmelite imagination constructing a myth. The role of myth is always valuable, and in a religious context myth has profound significance. It is the way the community reflects on its key experiences that shapes them so that the experience can then be handed on as a formative story:

> In this work we are able to observe the medieval Carmelite imagination at work in the construction of a myth. This myth expresses the order's sense of the nature and purpose of its vocation in the church and gives imaginative form to the values and aspirations which it wished to see expressed in its life as a religious community. Its principal building blocks are the Scriptures, which are ingeniously interpreted to construct a continuous history of the 'Elijah institute' over the centuries from the time of its foundation by the prophet until his followers were converted to Christianity. Our first reaction may be to laugh at this apparent naivete, but a more careful and sympathetic reading will show a profound spiritual dynamic at work. The essential elements and ideals of Carmelite life – the

inspiration of the Spirit, the opening of the heart and mind to the Messiah, the dynamic of communal discernment, the importance of the word of God, and much else besides – are projected into the past and given concrete 'mythic' form. Once we have the key to interpreting these stories, we can see unfold the spiritual itinerary of the Carmelite and the inner dynamic and central values of the Carmelite vocation.[3]

The *Institute* is divided into seven books of eight chapters. The key text is God's command to Elijah to go and hide in the brook Cherith (1 Kings 17:3-4). It is this command and the journey that follows which create the central theme of the work. There are two journeys – one where Elijah is transformed by love and the other the historical development of the Order as the Sons of the Prophets.

I would like to concentrate on Book 1 of the *Institute* where Elijah is shown as the model of monastic life and also, as a consequence, a model for Carmelites. The *Institute* is presented as a dialogue between John, 44th Bishop of Jerusalem in the fourth century, and the monk Caprasius. Caprasius is asking about the origins of the Order. He is introduced to the life and works of Elijah. Elijah is seen as the first leader of the monks from whom 'the holy and ancient institute took its origin'.

Elijah is commanded by God to go and hide himself in the valley to embrace solitude. The text that is taken as the basis for this withdrawal, and so becomes a key text, is from the First Book of Kings: 'The word of Yahweh came to him, "Go away from here, go eastwards, and hide yourself in the Wadi Cherith which lies east of Jordan. You can drink from the stream, and I have ordered the ravens to bring you food there" ' (1 Kings 17:2-4 JB).

The author asks us to reflect on these words in what he calls their mystical sense, by which he means that he is interested in showing how the prophet and then the reader can be transformed by love. We should try to achieve a pure heart, that is, we should avoid anything that is not inspired by love, and it is when we are hidden in Cherith that we can achieve this. If we do achieve a pure undivided heart, then even in this life we can experience something of the divine presence and heavenly glory. We shall drink of the torrent of the presence of God. However, in order to achieve a pure heart there is a need to follow four steps so as to ascend to the peak of perfection and be able to drink of the torrent.

The first step is renunciation of earthly things. As one reads the *Institute* it is easy to see that much of what is said sounds familiar. The vision, the full expression of it all, will appear in the works of Teresa of Avila and John of the Cross. They in their turn had the *Institute* as part of their formation. These are the holy Fathers of our Order that Teresa mentions in her writings. John of the Cross, with his teaching about '*todo*' ('all') and '*nada*' ('nothing'), is obviously expressing the essence of the sense of renunciation that the *Institute* calls for, while the torrent of the presence of God is expressed in John's vision of the mystical union of spiritual marriage.

For the author of the *Institute*, possession of riches does not close the gate to the Kingdom. It is rather a matter of what we set our heart on. However, once we have possessions, the worries and anxieties they bring are like weeds choking the growth of a plant. But then he asks, what are riches compared to the gift of eternal life? This short passage on our attitude to possessions is a marvellous weaving together of comment and passages from Wisdom literature and the Gospels.

The next step is the renunciation of sin and self-will. Here the key concept is that we must take up the cross and enter into the Passion of Christ so that we can come to resurrection, to a new purified life. The image for change is that of the journey 'towards the East' to the Wadi Cherith – in the opposite direction of our desires. The key example of renunciation of self-will is Jesus who came from heaven to do the Father's will and who stripped himself of glory. Jesus becomes the model here so that asceticism is rooted in his saving actions and in his spirit of loving obedience.

The third step to perfection is silence, solitude and celibacy. Here the author sounds somewhat like Nicholas the Frenchman, who saw the city and crowds of people as hostile to growth in perfection. On the other hand, given the overall tenor of the work, the ideal of solitude is stressed as a value even for those who are working among the people. There is also a realisation of human frailty and the need to gather ourselves together rather than be fragmented by business. Celibacy is counselled as an ideal that goes with seeking the Kingdom as the primary value. It is not a denial of relationships, but rather implies that giving oneself to God is the most powerful of dynamics. Silence in this context is vital for a dialogue with God as it creates the condition for listening. Likewise in a community setting, silence symbolises respect for others and their needs and is a genuine antidote to superficiality in relationships.

The fourth step to perfection is growth in love. To be in Cherith, which means love, is the ideal. This is the gospel call to us to give our whole being unreservedly to God. Again the call is for purity of heart so that the only object of love is God. However, the writer stresses that such a pure love will mean loving our neighbour, as the sincerity of our love is shown when we love our brothers and sisters. If we do not love those we can see, how can we love the God we do not see? The other love we must have is of ourselves, because if we are lovable to God then we need to value ourselves. God is the source of our joy and our being. If we live in this threefold love then we will also find forgiveness, because the more we love then the more we will find and live forgiveness. The vision that emerges from this section shows us how love sets us free for loving service and how, by our very being with others, we will do good.

These four steps should bring us to the experience of perfect love. This experience is described as drinking from the stream. It becomes possible when we are purified and offer no obstacle in our hearts to union with God. The writer promises that

those who cling to him with a pure heart will enjoy as

their reward an abundance of divine conversation so that hidden and even future things will be revealed to you by God. Then you will abound in unspeakable delights and shall gladly lift up the face of your mind to contemplate God.[4]

This closeness to God is not meant to be a continuous state – it is a gift and a grace. The awareness of God's closeness will come and go so that we do not become complacent, but more to the point, the more we long for that closeness, the more intense the union, the experience, will become. However, in the intervening periods we will be fed by God's word by his prophets. In this passage it is possible to see the seeds of John of the Cross's teaching on the Dark Night – the sense that we are called to a light beyond the lights we have known.

O Light Invisible, we praise thee!
Too bright for mortal vision.
O Greater Light, we praise Thee for the less;
The eastern light our spires touch at morning.
The light that slants upon our western doors at evening,
The twilight over stagnant pools at batflight,
Moon light and star light, owl and moth light,
Glow-worm glowlight on a grassblade.
O Light Invisible, we worship Thee!

We thank Thee for the lights that we have kindled,
The light of altar and of sanctuary;
Small lights of those who meditate at midnight
And lights directed through the coloured panes of
  windows
And light reflected from the polished stone,
The gilded carven wood, the coloured fresco.
Our gaze is submarine, our eyes look upward
And see the light that fractures through unquiet water.
We see the light but see not whence it comes.
O Light Invisible, we glorify Thee!

T. S. Eliot[5]

The second book of the *Institute* presents Elijah as the perfect model of the religious life. The first book looked at the spiritual meaning of the scriptural text. Now the historical sense is taken up. Elijah the first monk or hermit is presented to us. This section begins to weave scriptural and patristic texts reflecting on Elijah as the first monk. One authority, the Scriptures, is supported by another, the Fathers. Elijah is seen as dying to the flesh (Romans 7) and imitating the angels in his purity. Isidore, Jerome and Cassian are all quoted to testify that Elijah was the first to practise the virtue of chastity. St John Chrysostom praises him for his poverty: 'How was Elijah marvellous? – in his renunciation of possessions.' He was also totally available to the will of God in the service of his people. Again he is praised for his repentance, dying to sin so that he is ready to be open to God. His encounters with God deepen his ardour and enable him to trust evermore in God's providence. This leads him to a wisdom, a sense of discernment, qualifying him to be master of his disciples.

Paul Chandler observes that while the biblical Elijah is a mysterious and solitary person who appears from the desert and then leaves in the fiery chariot, this is not the picture painted in the Carmelite tradition. In the Carmelite working of the Elijah myth, he is the founder and father of a growing community of disciples. The first Carmelites did not simply take the biblical story about Elijah, but reflected on it and linked it to their story. Such a reading of the Scripture is not one that fits in with twentieth-century Scripture studies, but it was a lived experience for the medieval Carmelite. The text, like any written text, is always open to interpretation, and the relation between reader and text has its own special dynamism.

Book VI of the *Institute* links the Elijan and Marian traditions of the Order. Early references speak of the church on Mount Carmel being dedicated to Mary and papal documents speak of the hermit brothers of Mary of Mount Carmel. In 1282 when the Prior General, Peter Milau, wrote to Edward I of England asking for his support on behalf of the Order he spoke of the Order being founded in honour of Mary. The constitutions of 1324 add a paragraph to the rubric giving the Elijan origin: 'After the Incarnation their successors built a Church there (on Mount Carmel) in honour of the Blessed Virgin Mary and chose her title; therefore from that time they were by apostolic privilege called the Brothers of B.V.M. of Mount Carmel.'[6]

This reference to the successors of the prophets building a church on Carmel in early Christian times is the beginning of the weaving of Mary into the myth of Carmelite origins. John Baconthorpe (d. 1348), who was one of the first notable Carmelite theologians, a native of Blakeney in Norfolk, wrote at length about Mary and Carmel. Over and above his theological interest in Mary, he was a great defender of the Order and its position. He was the first to see the small cloud of 1 Kings 18:44 as a symbol of Mary: 'The servant said, "Now there is a cloud, small as a man's hand, rising from the sea" ' (JB). Baconthorpe saw Mary as the one who enables the rains of mercy and grace to restore all things. As she was in harmony with God she could be a means of God's grace to her brothers and sisters. Ribot takes the vision on Carmel of the little cloud that ends the drought as a way of drawing Elijah and Mary together. Mary is the cloud of pure rain rising from the salty sea. The salty sea is an image of sinful humanity.

Christopher O'Donnell, in an unpublished article on Mary in the Carmelite tradition, gives a helpful synthesis of Book VI of the *Institute*:

> The main Marian treatment is in Book Six. Throughout this book Ribot is concerned with the Order's title, 'Brothers of the Blessed Virgin Mary of Mount Carmel'; he also allows that 'Carmelites' is a legitimate title. A fundamental idea which he developed was a spiritual, somewhat arbitrary interpretation of the little cloud seen by Elijah (see 1 Kings 18:44). The key to its Marian symbolism is that the cloud of pure rain, that is Mary, arose from the bitter, salty sea, which is the image of sinful

humanity. The prophet received by divine illumination four mysteries about the future redemption of the human race which he communicated to his followers: 1. the birth of the future redeemer from a virgin-mother who from her origin would be free from any stain of sin; 2. the time when this would be accomplished; 3. the deliberate decision of the future mother to keep herself always a virgin, consecrated to the service of the Lord; 4. the fecundity of her virginity, foreshadowed by the rain, which would relieve the condition of humankind.

In imitation of Elijah who was the first Old Testament virgin, Mary would vow virginity and be the first woman to do so. The successors of Elijah also took such a vow. This established a similitude and a deep empathy between them and Mary so that they called her their sister and themselves Brothers of the Blessed Virgin Mary. The notion of sister does not, however, eliminate the word 'mother', which is delicately insinuated: 'Before he (the Word) was incarnated there was only a fraternity of paternity, because from the same Father of whom the Son was eternally generated, was also created the human race ... before he was incarnated there was not a fraternity of maternity, since the Son was not yet born of his mother.' The implication is that after the Incarnation, there was a new basis of fraternity in the motherhood of Mary.

The by now traditional title of 'Patron' is allied also with virginity. The Carmelites took care to serve the Virgin with special devotion. They were eager specially to choose this virgin as a patron for themselves, because they knew that she alone was singularly like them in the first-fruits of spontaneous virginity. For just as spontaneous virginity for God was first begun by the ancient followers of this religion and introduced to men, so the same virginity was afterwards first introduced and begun among women by the Mother of God.

Thus we see in Ribot a synthesis through virginity of

the traditional notions of Mary and the Order – Mother, Patron and Sister. And all of these ultimately stemmed from the author's contemplation of the spiritual meaning of the little cloud. However, it is not so much that Ribot is adding something new to the Order's Marian consciousness; he reads into the little cloud what was the Order's attitude to Mary, but gave more clearly than previous writers its basis as virginity. Indeed, he uses a false etymology for the word 'Carmel' to indicate 'knowledge of circumcision' which he then interprets as virginity for God, sought first by Elijah and his followers, and then by Mary.[7]

Ribot is as anxious as Baconthorpe to defend the validity of the Marian titles of the Order and, like Baconthorpe in his myth-making, articulates the Order's consciousness of being in the service of Mary.

The *Institute* was a key text for medieval Carmelites and continued as such into the sixteenth century. The stories told about Elijah and the virtues practised by the prophet and his disciples represented a Carmelite Utopia. These values and aspirations became, for fourteenth-century Carmelites, the model for their way of life. It is useful to list the ideals of Elijah, as these Carmelites saw them:

1. faithfulness to the Word of God;
2. total availability to the will of God in the service of his people;
3. knowledge of the truth about this world;
4. solitude, which is an option for God above all else;
5. not only repentance for personal sins, but intercession for the sins of others;
6. living the life of love, and so he is a mystic drinking from 'the stream of delight', with the fire of divine love burning in his heart;
7. a total trust in the Providence of God, an awareness that God cares for those who seek first God's Kingdom and its justice;
8. a loving wisdom that comes from his closeness to God;

9. a sense of care and responsibility towards his disciples.

The Carmelite tradition about Elijah was rich and complex. For the medieval mind he was seen more and more as the model for religious life. The *Institute* shows Elijah moving from the solitary to be ever more at the centre of a community of disciples who live after his example.

The *Institute* places great emphasis on the text where Elijah goes East to hide in Cherith. However, towards the end of the work another text is used which has a central importance. It is the passage from Acts 2 that speaks of the Jerusalem community: 'They remained faithful to the teaching of the apostles, to the brotherhood, to the breaking of the bread.' This vision of the apostolic community at Jerusalem as an ideal is very much part of the Rule. Appearing where it does in the *Institute*, it seems like the second pillar or foundation of the Carmelite life. The Carmelite meditates, comes to Eucharist with a burning heart and, strengthened by the Risen Christ, can go out and be ready for mission.

The *Institute* enabled generations of Carmelites to have both a vision of their origins and a dynamic for the present. Sadly, in the seventeenth century attention became focused on trying to prove the historical element in the book. Endless efforts went on in a controversy whereby enthusiasts tried to establish an actual lineage from Elijah to the first Carmelites in the twelfth century. The project was flawed, the understanding of the myth was lost and it has been only in the last few decades that the value and meaning of the text has been grasped again. What we do know is the fact that John of the Cross and Teresa of Avila were nourished by the *Institute* and found in it seeds of inspiration for their project.

4. THE TRADITION AT RISK

The years from the Black Death to the Reformation were an uneasy time for religious orders. The great plague affected the social fabric of Europe and the resulting tensions were damaging for the life of the Church and the Order. The divisions in the Church that resulted from the Avignon Captivity and the schisms it engendered touched every religious order. Conflicting jurisdictions undermined authority, observance in religious orders suffered. Privileges and dispensations that could be obtained from kings and popes cut through the sense of fraternity in community. The non-observance of poverty became a source of scandal that was far worse than sexual laxity. Monks and friars gradually lost their popular support and in an unequal society they could be seen as yet another burden on the poor.

The Carmelites were part of this late medieval society and by 1400 were fully integrated into the mendicant movement. Were they all as ripe for criticism as Chaucer's friar or did the idealism of the Rule and the *Institute* still inspire commitment? Certainly in England the fifteenth century dawned with a number of friars who are remembered for their learning and involvement in the life of the Spirit. The Provincial of the time, Thomas Netter (1370–1430), was a distinguished theologian and a vigorous upholder of Carmelite values. He was much in demand in the public domain, but was most concerned with the well-being of the Order. Many of his contemporaries were theologians often locked in combat with the Wycliffites, but others like Richard Misyn and Thomas Fishlake were linked to the mystics of the day. Thomas Fishlake translated Walter

Hilton's *The Scale of Perfection* into Latin. Richard Misyn, who was Prior at Lincoln, but who also for a time lived as a hermit, translated the works of Richard Rolle into English. He translated the *De Emendatione Vitae* in 1434 and *Incendium Amoris* in 1435. (*The Fire of Love* and *The Mending of Life* were published by the Early English Texts Society in 1896.) Other writers of the period who helped through their love of Scripture and their willingness to communicate with their contemporaries were friars like Richard of Maidstone and John Pascal who became Bishop of Llandaff.

Robert Southfield, who was a member of the community at Norwich, had a reputation as a mystic and spiritual director. Margery Kempe went to see him and Dame Julian. He believed that the Holy Ghost was working powerfully in Margery's soul. Alan of Lynn was also well known as a spiritual guide, but his Provincial forbade him to have anything to do with Margery Kempe. Another friar from Norwich, Thomas Scrope, was famous for his apocalyptic preaching. He eventually lived as a hermit near to the Norwich Priory, but was called from his solitude to be a bishop. He exercised a conscientious ministry in South East England and found time to translate Ribot's *Institutio Primorum Monachorum* into English.

The fact that the fifteenth-century English Province produced these friars indicates a faithfulness to the Order's basic vision. Moreover they were not only men of prayer, but keen to enable their contemporaries to have access to works of spiritual substance in the vernacular.

The Order was also fortunate to have clear leadership from John Soreth who was Prior General from 1451–1471. John Soreth came from Caen and while he was a young friar his community was under the jurisdiction of the English Province as Henry V had re-conquered Normandy. He was a vigorous reformer and worked to ensure that the Rule was observed regarding poverty and the spirit of prayer. His work for reform bore its greatest fruits in Northern Europe, and he was also able to support the Mantuan reform in Italy. This reform, based in Northern Italy, was an attempt to combat laxity and uphold observance. A later result of his work was the reform of Albi which had a positive influence in France. A guiding light of this reform was William McGregor, a Scot, who was a Doctor of Theology from the Sorbonne.

John Soreth must also be remembered as the Prior General who enabled the female side of Carmel to take root. The Bull *Cum Nulla* authorised the receiving of women into the Order and soon convents sprang up in Northern France, Belgium, Italy and Spain. Frances of Amboise, the widow of the Duke of Brittany, was a keen supporter of John's work in establishing these convents. She eventually became a Carmelite and abandoned all privileges, happy to be a sister among her sisters. Soreth saw the setting up of convents for women as part of his reform and he hoped that the prayerful structures he had created would be an impetus to better observance among the friars. Soreth's reforms and his love of the Rule was a vital moment in Carmel's story, but the Order had to wait until Nicholas Audet to find another Prior General of vision.

The fifteenth century was also the beginning of the Renaissance and, while it is not the purpose of this study to give a total view of the Carmelite story, it is important to remember that many friars were distinguished humanists. Painters, musicians, poets all flourished in the Order. Fra Filippo Lippi, while not exemplary as a religious, is one of the great Renaissance painters, and Baptist of Mantua was called the Christian Virgil. Shakespeare refers to him as 'O Blessed Mantuan'. John Holby and William of Worcester made their mark as musicians, spending much of their lives in Italy. A centre of Christian humanism in Denmark was the Carmelite College in Copenhagen. Its regent Paul Helie was very much in the mould of John Colet, Dean of St Paul's in London, and was a great admirer of Erasmus.

The Order had to wait for some fifty years for positive leadership. This came from Nicholas Audet. Audet was to be General from 1524 until his death in 1562. He was born in Cyprus, so his links with the Holy Land were strong, and because of the island's link with Venice that city was to become his second home. Audet did not seek high office, but he was eager to work for reform. He believed in living a genuine community life, he valued studies and he saw initial formation as vital. Renewal was his programme and he pursued that programme with vigour. He travelled widely and where he was unable to go he sent delegates to promulgate his reforms. His work was hampered by the Reformation (in which seven provinces were lost to the Order) and also by internal strife. Another negative factor was the Roman Curia, which often gave friars privileges and dispensations that undermined his efforts. Audet was also involved in the Council of Trent and its subsequent reform programme. However, he did have a good degree of success with his own programme of internal reform and by 1550 the provinces of Castile and Portugal were classed as Observant. (For a Province to be Observant meant, above all, that poverty was lived in each of the communities and privileges flowing from academic achievement were curtailed.) With Audet's death a long chapter in the Order's story closes, and waiting in the wings to revitalise Carmel are key figures who, for some, have come to dominate the whole story. Rather, they should be seen as immensely gifted Carmelites who brought a new energy, but remain a part of the whole picture of Carmel.

5. THE MYSTIC WAY

The inspiration of the Carmelite Order is a single-hearted following of Jesus Christ by a group of poor brothers. Prayer and simplicity of life are at the heart of the Carmelite project. Medieval Carmelites were constantly recalled to their origins and all the projects of reform focused on fidelity to prayer and a sincere practice of community life. However, legislation and exhortation could never effect renewal. What was needed was a renewal of the original vision and inspiration, something that would stir the imagination.

The sixteenth-century Spanish mystics, Teresa of Avila and John of the Cross, provided the impetus for renewal in Carmel and also left a wonderful legacy for Christianity as a whole. They represent both continuity and a way forward in the Carmelite story.

The sixteenth century was an age of upheaval, discovery and change. It was the century of the Reformation and the time when Europeans ventured out to explore the Americas and the Indies. It was the century of the High Renaissance when the arts flourished and modern science emerged. In Spain the Moors (North African Muslims) had been expelled after an occupation of many centuries, and this was an era of Christian power and expansion. It was a time when national unity was being established, and under the reign of Philip II a climate of political and religious control became a part of life. The control exercised by the Inquisition, more an arm of the State than of the Church, would cast a shadow over the lives of both John and Teresa.

The reforms of John Soreth and Nicholas Audet prepared

the way for John and Teresa. John Soreth's encouragement had enabled Carmelite communities of women to flourish and the establishment of the Convent of the Incarnation of Avila in the early sixteenth century was a result of that policy. The reforms that Soreth and Audet introduced meant that the Carmelite friars in Castile were observant and open to positive inspirations. The ideals expressed in the *Institute* were being taught in Spain so there was vitality and enthusiasm.

It is also interesting that both Teresa and John, to use a modern term, were 'disadvantaged' and were therefore in a special way already poor. Neither Teresa nor John possessed *limpieza de sangre* – 'purity of blood'. They had Jewish fore-bears, and this ancestry was viewed with suspicion and could be the reason for persecution. By the end of the sixteenth century religious orders in Spain had made *limpieza de sangre* a condition for admission. Fortunately the Carmelites did not put such legislation into place until 1596.

Teresa de Ahumada y Cepeda was born in Avila in 1515. Her grandfather on her father's side, Juan Sanchez, was a convert Jew from Toledo. He came to the authorities' notice, because after his conversion he decided to return for a while to his original faith. This family history made life difficult for Teresa's father and she grew up aware of the crisis in her family. Teresa reacted to the situation by being open and forth-right in her dealings with those in authority. She entered the Convent of the Incarnation in Avila in 1535. Her life in the Incarnation was for some twenty years a time for search-ing, illness and bereavement. Her father's death in 1543 was an important moment, but her conversion experience came in Lent 1554 when she was touched to the core of her being at the realisation of Christ's suffering and wounded humanity.

At about this time Teresa was given a copy of St Augustine's *Confessions*, which had just been translated into Castilian. Reading about Augustine's conversion deepened her own sense of being opened to Christ and awakened her thirst for prayer. She began to feel the call to enter into an ever deeper com-munion with Christ. The next six years saw an abundance of rich, deep experiences of closeness to Christ. Teresa was fortunate to have a series of good spiritual directors who respected the work of the Holy Spirit in her life. Among her guides were several Jesuits and the Franciscan, St Peter of Alcántara. St Peter of Alcántara proved a valuable guide, helping Teresa to integrate the mystical experiences into her life. The sculptor Bernini was to celebrate one such experience with his famous statue that shows an angel piercing the heart of Teresa with a spear. The statue catches symbolically the sublime moment of divine union and is itself an amazing testimony to the saint.

In 1560 Teresa began to think about the possibility of beginning a reform in Carmel. She was conscious in the context of the Reformation that the Church needed renewal and that this should include renewal of religious communities. She was aware of the ideals of Carmel expressed in the Rule and the *Institute* and she was to sum up those ideals when she said:

> So I say now that all of us who wear this holy habit of Carmel are called to prayer and contemplation. This call explains our origin; we are descendants of men who felt this call, of those holy fathers on Mount Carmel who in such great solitude and contempt for the world sought this treasure, this precious pearl of contemplation that we are speaking about. Yet few of us dispose ourselves that the Lord may communicate it to us.[1]

The Convent of the Incarnation had its problems, but not because of any lack of commitment by the community. The Incarnation was too large and too busy, and lack of resources prevented community life from flourishing. Teresa wanted to restore the life of prayer in solitude – she wanted to find again what had been the essence of life on Mount Carmel. The new foundation was meant to be a picture of what the Order had been in its earliest days. Teresa wanted a small community bonded by friendship and simple in lifestyle so that financial problems would not overwhelm the life of poverty. Privilege and rank were to give way to a sense of family. It was for these sisters that Teresa began to write and to share her experiences of intimacy with Christ. She wrote her *Life* in 1562 and *The Way of Perfection* in 1565.

Her *Life* or autobiography was written in the first instance for her confessor. It combines accounts of her interior journey with autobiographical details. Teresa had a clear, direct style; she wrote as she spoke. She was open, even rugged. Now that we know more of her background and the struggles her family experienced because of their Jewish ancestry, it is no surprise that she has no patience with rank and favour. What you see and hear is the person she is. This directness is found in the way she comes to envisage prayer as 'nothing else than an intimate sharing between friends'.[2] However, as Teresa wrote about mental prayer – contemplation – she was aware that the Inquisition of her day was suspicious of mental prayer. Theologians like Melchior Cano lumped the contemplative life and Lutheran teaching together as dangerous. So when Teresa writes she does so against a background hostile to her dearest project. She also writes conscious that her confessor will read her work critically, given the climate of the time. To call her *Life* an autobiography could be misleading. True, there are facts about her life, but such information is scattered and fragmentary. What is of the essence is the story of an inner journey. It is vital in our understanding both of Teresa and of ourselves.

For Teresa the inner journey is one where the love and mercy of God transform her. However, she does this while being very conscious that the way forward is to allow her humanity to be transformed and linked to the humanity of Christ. She is quite blunt in opposing those who would intellectualise prayer. 'We are not angels, we have a body.' Teresa was a person who had a gift for friendship, and it was this gift that was lifted up and transformed through her understanding that Jesus Christ was her good friend. Teresa wants to spend time with that friend in a conversation which is for her the best way of prayer. The more she is in friendship, the more God's mercy and grace water the garden of her being. Like the picture of Elijah in the *Institute*, she drinks from the source of God's love. Her friendship with Christ is so vivid to her that he is wonderful company, always at our side as we journey. She journeys to the spiritual summit which is union with Christ, and it is to this summit that Teresa believes all are called. Teresa has the sense that what she experiences in prayer, the mercy, the friendship, intimacy with Christ, should be normal for all of us. We will experience dryness. We will feel absence. Yet in these experiences we are being drawn out of ourselves to a new stage of union.

Teresa wrote with frankness. She was not a theologian and never pretended to be one. She was not a biblical scholar and access to the Bible was not easy, as even Latin versions of the Scriptures were not readily available, let alone a Spanish translation. However, she was conscious of God giving her words and she felt that her experience and her testimony had a validity, and was happy to share them. This desire to help others in their journey, especially her sisters in St Joseph, is the inspiration behind *The Way of Perfection*. It is meant to be a help in teaching her sisters to pray and reflects where Teresa had reached in her journey. As a Carmelite she was committed to following Christ, being in allegiance to him, given over to her Lord. In the greater solitude of St Joseph's, where she could live out Chapter 7 of the Rule, pondering God's word, she became ever more open to receive Christ in the most profound way, so that more and more Christ could be everything for her. He becomes for her the teacher of prayer who enables us to pray to the Father from the depth of our being. Images abound in her writings, many of them coming from Carmelite sources, like springs of living water and the reality of spiritual warfare. The Rule and the Elijah myth provide the framework, the original inspiration.

Teresa wrote *The Way of Perfection* at a time when her whole project of reform and teaching was being received in a rather negative fashion. She and her sisters, because they were women, were regarded as unreliable by theologians. Teresa found these attitudes painful and she could be outspoken against them. It is this directness that gives her writing a sense of freshness for the contemporary reader. At times also Teresa is ironical, sounding like a more uninhibited Jane Austen; no wonder she was admired by George Eliot.

Teresa was never an organised, schematic writer; her writings come from her warmth, her experience. However, she does give clear guidelines and her themes emerge with a boldness of expression. She is aware from her own conversion experience of the need to grow from a solid human basis. Prayer comes from a life of practical love, from detachment and humility. We cannot talk to God if we do not speak lovingly to our neighbour and we need realism, and a grounding of our lives.

Love of neighbour means friendship, and the warmth of human friendship is Teresa's keynote. An essential part of her reform was to create communities where the human dimension was respected and where the sisters lived in friendship. Teresa opposed social pretension and knew from her own family's experience how distorted notions of honour, status and race were damaging and unchristian. Her communities were truly sisterhoods where people could live accepting each other and growing through an intimate sharing of life.

Friendship with God and entry into the life of the Trinity is the end of the journey in *The Way of Perfection*. Teresa is conscious of the nearness of God, the one who takes the initiative. Again it is the humanity of Christ as found in the Gospels that is the way for Teresa. Christ is the teacher and the 'Our Father' is the great prayer that he gives us. For Teresa, to pray this prayer with recollection, allowing it to be the starting point for contemplation, is to make it the gateway to closeness with God. Then in the closeness to God through Christ we are nourished with springs of living water.

It was at this stage in her life in 1567 that Teresa encountered John Baptist Rossi, the Prior General of the Order, who was visiting the Spanish Provinces. Rossi was eager to continue the project of Reform that his predecessor Nicholas Audet had begun. However, while Rossi was committed to structural reform, Teresa's project offered something that went far beyond legal prescriptions. She wanted the following of Christ with an undivided heart, the vision of the 'way of life' of Albert. Teresa was nervous when she met the Prior General, thinking he might be angry with her or send her back to the Incarnation Convent. The opposite was true, as Rossi saw that Teresa had vision and her way had a significance for the whole Order. He took her work under his jurisdiction and encouraged its propagation. Rossi was to write to Teresa urging her to found as many convents as there were hairs on her head. They established a deep respect for each other – in fact he was to write in 1569 to the nuns at Medina Del Campo, saying:

> I give infinite thanks to the Divine Majesty for the great favour bestowed on this Order by the diligence and goodness of Our Reverend Mother Teresa of Jesus. She profits the Order more than all the friars in Spain. I admonish all to obey the above mentioned Teresa as a true superior and a jewel to be much valued as precious and a friend of God.[3]

The continuing support that Rossi gave Teresa was a source of joy to her:

> He wrote to me about every house that we have founded and it gave him the keenest pleasure that the foundations in question were being made. Really the greatest relief I had in all my trials was to see what joy this gave him for I felt that in affording it to him I was serving our Lord as he was my superior and quite apart from this I have a great love for him.[4]

Teresa worked to the end of her life founding convents, the last in Burgos in 1582, the year of her death. *The Book of Foundations*, written in 1577, tells the story of this work set in the context of her powerful sense of the presence of God in all that she was doing. Rossi's support and friendship gave Teresa great encouragement. He had been quick to grasp the creativity and imagination behind Teresa's vision. It was this sort of energy that the Prior General saw as being of the essence of any renewal of the Order. Rossi hoped this vision would percolate through the Order. However, despite all he did in Spain, interference from the king and various bishops in later years was to bring the Reform into conflict with the central authority of the Order. Misunderstandings would cause suffering and those who were most idealistic would suffer most.

In the midst of her work of founding convents Teresa found time to write *The Interior Castle*. It could be called an essay on the spiritual life written by a mystic. This is a book about the journey to the centre, to that point where we have the fullest communion with God. Teresa begins by pointing out the dangers of delusion and fantasy. Also, while she herself experienced visions she does not lay great store by them. The key image is that of the Castle: like a diamond or shining glass it has many facets or 'rooms', but the goal is its very centre. In the Castle we see God and through God we begin to discover our true self. We should want to move on so that we can become more open to God. The key is the desire to move forward, not being satisfied with where we are, and to risk passing through states of being that are beyond our control. Teresa can be exuberant with her imagery, but her wish is to show that we can find union with God. She does believe that there can be consummation or mystical marriage. Until we reach God, she believes, we are subject to discontent, and the only thing that will heal our restlessness is union with God. We need to surrender ourselves to the mystery of the presence of God that is at the core of our being. The heart cannot find rest and we are always yearning, looking for the love who is hidden, searching for the one who is so beautiful. The union Teresa speaks about is the union John of the Cross sings of in his poetry. Perhaps at this stage it is appropriate to say something more of John of the Cross, to see how he and Teresa interacted.

John was some twenty-five years younger than Teresa, and was born in Fontiveros in Castile in the very heart of Spain. He did not have an easy childhood as his parents came from opposite sides of the social divide. His father, Gonzalo de Yepes, came from a prosperous merchant family who lived in Toledo. However, like Teresa's family they were *conversos*, Jewish converts to Christianity, though many generations back. Gonzalo married a weaver, Catalina Alvarez, who was probably of Moorish descent. Gonzalo's family opposed the marriage and disowned their son. Tragedy struck the young family as Gonzalo died when John was only three. Catalina was left to bring up three young boys while working long hours weaving cloth. She moved to Medina del Campo, a busy market town, where she found a good outlet for her work. As a lone parent Catalina struggled against the odds, yet marvellous bonds of loyalty and love grew up between her and the boys. After some basic education, John worked at a local hospital as a nursing assistant. Many of the patients were dying of contagious diseases and John proved immensely caring. He loved music and often made music to help the dying feel loved. The hospital chaplain recognised John's gifts and enabled him to study at the newly established Jesuit College in Medina. For three years he studied literature, the classics and philosophy. Here he had his literary formation – the poet-to-be learning his craft. In 1563 John joined the Carmelite Community at Medina. Why did he choose the Carmelites? Perhaps because some of his father's family had been Carmelites belonging to the priory at Toledo. There were not many Carmelites in Castile, but we do know that they were observant and were to prove open to reform. It was after a period of study at Salamanca University that the newly ordained friar met Teresa at Avila in 1567. At this stage he was searching for a more contemplative way of life and was thinking of becoming a Carthusian. Teresa was impressed by the shy young friar and persuaded him to go back to Salamanca to finish his studies. She commented on John, making play about his height: 'Though he is small in stature he is great in God's eyes.'

When John had finished his studies in 1568 Teresa approached the superior of the Carmelite friars in Castile, Alonzo Gonzalez, and asked him to allow some of his friars to live according to her renewed vision or Reform. In the first instance she wanted friars who would help her nuns by hearing confessions and giving them guidance. John was willing to join in the project, as was Antonio de Heredia, who had been in charge of forming new members of the Order. However, Teresa wanted to make it clear that her reform was not meant to be superficial – something measured by austerity and ascetic practices. She wanted a balanced way of living in which charity, detachment and humility mattered more than spectacular penances. Her view of reform had nothing in common with short sharp shocks. Teresa was interested in creating environments where genuine humanity could flourish. She was to show John that what was vital was the development of the creative, the imaginative, in the life of a Christian. She helped him see that academic life had overshadowed the playful, creative side of his nature. His love of music, of poetry and storytelling were rediscovered and became central in his development. While John grew as a great teacher of the mystical life, it was his creative gifts that enabled him to communicate his profound experiences.

A new way of life began for John on 28 November 1568 at Duruelo, a small village between Avila and Salamanca. On that day he, Antonio and Joseph, the third member of the group, celebrated Mass presided over by the head of the Carmelite Order in Castile, Alonzo Gonzalez. The three friars put on habits made of coarse cloth and promised to live by a vision of Carmelite life that would reflect its early years on Mount Carmel. They wanted to turn their backs on any mitigation of the original Rule of the Order. To mark this moment as decisive, John took a new name and was henceforth known as John of the Cross. This way of life eventually gained the title of the Discalced Reform, the term 'discalced' meaning barefoot. Walking barefoot was a sign of reform in religious communities in the sixteenth century. In the case of these Carmelites, however, it meant wearing rough sandals.

The first priory of the 'Reform' was an old barn that the friars turned into a simple dwelling. John was delighted at the development – living this simple prayerful life fulfilled his heart's desire. There was another reason for John to be happy, as his mother volunteered to act as cook, while his brother Francisco came over to help in the restoration of the building. John never lost close links with his family, loving to spend time with them.

The new way of life, or Reform, began to spread with the foundation of new priories. John was soon called to leave Duruelo to help care for the young friars who were studying for ordination at Alcalá near Madrid. This was a role that John relished, as he had come to realise that the whole person had to be developed. Academic attainment was essential but these young men needed to value the traditions of the Order and be well grounded in humanity if they were to help people.

In 1572 John was sent to be confessor to the nuns at the Incarnation, where Teresa had been appointed Prioress. John worked with Teresa helping to achieve creative change in what was a large and varied community. He showed immense wisdom and tact in his dealings with the nuns, recognising each person's uniqueness. These five years in Avila were a time of mutual enrichment for John and Teresa. By this time Teresa was deeply advanced in the mystical life; she lived with a sense of God's closeness to her. She shared many of her insights and experiences with John, helping him in his turn make sense of the profound things happening in his life. Their friendship was a precious gift and perhaps can teach us today to value creative intimacy. John and Teresa were obviously attracted to each other, but in a way that respected each other's roles and journeys in life.

During this period in Avila, John, as ever, had time for the poor and disadvantaged. He was always ready to preach and spend time listening to people, especially the sick. He also remembered his own impoverished childhood and found time to teach poor children the basics of reading and writing. And, as always, he found time for his mother and brother as these were the most precious links in his life.

In 1577 John's life was turned upside down by events outside his control. Interference by the king and bad communications conspired to provoke serious misunderstanding between the Reformed Friars and the Observant Friars in Castile. The General in Rome believed his wishes were being ignored. In the middle of this conflict John became the innocent victim and was arrested on charges of gross disobedience. He was imprisoned in the priory at Toledo and was held in miserable conditions for some nine months, until he escaped. By 1581 the tensions had diminished, but John had suffered terribly. However, during this tragic, cruel time John had had profound religious experiences which he was able to express in sublime poetry. The long months of imprisonment brought him close to God and saw the awakening of a great artistic gift.

Despite the dark, the self-doubt and depression that must have gripped him in prison, John had an amazing experience of closeness to God; so close as to be akin to a physical union. John wanted to share this experience and the result is his poetry, which is among the finest in the Spanish language.

John's deep sense of union with the Divine is often called mystical. It was, as the *Institute* had said, a tasting of the reality of God even in this life. If anyone wants to learn from John of the Cross, it is important to approach him in the first place through his poetry and then to peruse the long prose commentaries. His poems are wonderful lyrical pieces written with great economy of style. John said that he did not have to search for words and images – they just came. Certainly the 'Dark Night' and the 'Spiritual Canticle' reflect his reading of Scripture and above all his love of the Song of Songs. This is a poetic book of the Bible that sings of the beauty and goodness of human loving. It is rich in imagery and is not afraid to be sensuous and erotic. The poetry is totally open in its celebration of sexual love, but is in no way prurient. The 'Dark Night' and the 'Spiritual Canticle' speak of the yearning of the lover's heart for the beloved. The gaze of God, the beloved, wounds the lover, who then can only find satisfaction when healed by loving union. This desire for God that can only be fulfilled by union echoes the Rule, and the sense of journeying is like Elijah moving to the east, to the source of life at Cherith.

Rather than talk about John's poetry it is better to let John speak for himself. For this purpose the poem 'The Dark Night' would be a good choice. The text and translation comes from *The Collected Works of St John of the Cross*, edited and translated by Kieran Kavanaugh and Otilio Rodriguez. This 1991 edition is published by the Institute of Carmelite Studies in Washington.

THE DARK NIGHT

Songs of the soul that rejoices in having reached the high state of perfection, which is union with God, by the path of spiritual negation.

1. One dark night,
   fired with love's urgent longings
   – ah, the sheer grace! –
   I went out unseen,
   my house being now all stilled.

2. In darkness, and secure,
   by the secret ladder, disguised,
   ah, the sheer grace! –
   in darkness and concealment,
   my house being now all stilled.

3. On that glad night in secret,
   for no one saw me,
   nor did I look at anything
   with no other light or guide
   than the one that burned in my heart.

4. This guided me more surely than the light of noon
   to where he was awaiting me
   – him I knew so well –
   there in a place where no one appeared.

5. O guiding night!
   O night more lovely than the dawn!
   O night that has united

the Lover with his beloved,
transforming the beloved in her Lover.

6. Upon my flowering breast,
   which I kept wholly for him alone,
   there he lay sleeping,
   and I caressing him
   there in a breeze from the fanning cedars.

7. When the breeze blew from the turret,
   and I parted his hair,
   it wounded my neck with its gentle hand,
   suspending all my senses.

8. I abandoned and forgot myself,
   laying my face on my Beloved;
   all things ceased;
   I went out from myself,
   leaving my cares forgotten among the lilies.[5]

The key symbol used in the poem is that of the night – it is the darkness of John's prison cell, but it is also a time of mystery, a time to begin a journey that will lead to union with God. The night loses its menace because the lover trusts in the object of desire and finds a light in her heart that guides the lover to union. The union is beyond anything we could imagine and is expressed as a wound, because the intensity of such love seems painful. The finite human spirit overwhelmed by the infinite – it is the same state that Bernini expresses in his famous statue of Teresa's heart being wounded by the angel.

So the beloved, who stands for you and me as we journey to God, has found perfect union with God. The final stanza takes us to fulfilment and hints at the joy of heaven, the beatific vision. This state of union, where only God matters, is the mystic state and in this poem John believes that human beings can experience such closeness to God in this life. As the poem moves from the house to finding the Lover, it expresses a journey that is a wonderful risk. Perhaps John is trying to tell us that, because we image God in our humanity, then if we trust enough in who we are, we can be passionately close to God. This sense of trust is there in the closing lines:

> I went out from myself
> Leaving my cares
> forgotten among the lilies.

These lines link the poem by allusion to the Sermon on the Mount, where Christ uses the beauty of the lilies of the field to emphasise God's care for us and our need to trust in that care.

John wrote four great prose works. On one level they are commentaries on his poems, on another they offer us his vision of how we achieve union with God. The four works are *The Ascent of Mount Carmel*, *The Dark Night*, *Spiritual Canticle* and *The Living Flame of Love*. They were written between 1579 and 1586 and were intended to help the friars and nuns of the Reform. These works come from a mental universe that is very different from ours: it was still a world of faith, and for the nuns and friars their Carmelite Rule presented the following of Christ as a core value. Again, John uses scholastic terminology that needs a great deal of commentary. However, the heart of his message is that only God can satisfy our hunger and that even in the darkest times God's transcendence will emerge. A final comment: John's prose style is very difficult, as his sentences are long and, because he wrote when he had time, in between countless other tasks, his works are often repetitive.

John introduces the concept of the 'dark night' early on, as the way a person grows closer to God. He points out that what he has to say will not be easy and apologises for his 'awkward style'. He stresses he is writing for people who are already taking all this very seriously – the friars and nuns of the Reform.

We need to be quite clear that John saw the 'dark night' as initiated by God, but that does not mean that the individual person is totally passive in the process. Another aspect of the 'dark night' is the way a person so affected feels that God seems to be absent. It is important to recognise that this is a *seeming* absence of God – it is not as if God has indeed withdrawn from a person's life. Again it needs to be noted that not everyone in their journey to God passes through the 'dark night'. In an attempt to understand what John means by the 'dark night' the reader must always remember that whoever enters on this process has to play his or her part. John does not deny our basic freedom or our use of reason.

The way of the night is for John the way of *nada*. A time of faith and of purification, *nada* is an escape from all that is negative so that a person finds their all – *todo* – in God. The way of the night is both a process in which we can co-operate by positive creative practices, and also involves being open to God at work in us. It is a time of growing into maturity, but should be lived in a spirit of trust. However, once a person comes closer to God in faith, the new relationship makes it possible to live with greater humanity and to enjoy creation from a more positive perspective. In his own life John loved nature and had wonderful friendships. Most of his correspondence has been lost, but what survives reveals a man of warmth, loyalty and integrity. His closeness to God helped his growth in humanity.

Obviously the joy of coming into a close relationship with God is something that few people can articulate. John's poems do that through powerful symbols and because he was able to find words that surprised even him by their power. However, what stands out in his writings is the language he uses about our union with God. It is the language and images of the most tender and fulfilled human loving. This is powerful news for our own times because it tells us that human love at its most sublime is the best image we can find for the relationship between God and ourselves. It also suggests that we need some experience of human tenderness to set us on the journey to God. I believe that how we love each other and how we love God is reciprocal, each love effecting and enhancing the other. The journey into God that John shows us is a journey where possessiveness disappears and faith, trust and love find freedom to flourish. It is because a certain true human growth and freedom is realised that we can come close to God. If, however, we have grown to a true maturity in our innermost being, then we are able to relate in a way that is gentler, deeper and more understanding of the other.

John's life gave space and time to love and friendship. He felt a freedom in intimacy – he wanted neither to possess nor to be possessed. He could celebrate friendship and was honest in the joy such relations brought him. Because the mystics are open to the loving wisdom of God and allow the love of the Spirit freedom, they achieve a humanity that is creative, sensitive and spontaneous. Perhaps one of the great contributions that a teacher like John of the Cross could make for people today is that, in pointing to the way to grow in a loving trust of God and in the experience of unconditional love, he enables men and women to gain confidence in the possibility of achieving full loving relationships. Mysticism could well be a school for marriage.

There has never been more talk about relationships than today, and yet it would seem that there has never been greater difficulty in living them out. It appears we do not know what we want from each other and the hurt and the anger this causes is terrible. Can John's *nada* lead to a *todo* for people wanting to find love and deep relationships? I believe it can, because John will help us discover 'the other' in all their beauty, and he has much to say to the 'devices and desires' of our hearts.

John died in 1591, and by then the Reform was flourishing. Tensions continued to exist but now they arose from disagreements about the direction the Reform should take. Nicholas Doria, who was now in charge of the movement, tended towards a rigour that was not to John's liking. In fact the last year of John's life was overshadowed by conflicts in the Reform and by his ill-health. However, the vision and gifts that flowed from John and Teresa had renewed Carmel. Sadly the Reform was eventually to split from the parent body and become a separate order. What really matters, however, is that the

Church has been enriched through two great teachers in the life of the Spirit, gifted with imaginative power and wonderful humanity. It is good to note that contemporary Carmelites of both branches acknowledge how wonderfully Carmel was energised by these two saints. Today the Carmelite family is more conscious of its shared heritage than its past divisions in the sixteenth century.

6. OVERWHELMED BY GOD'S LOVING PRESENCE – JOHN OF ST SAMSON AND LAWRENCE OF THE RESURRECTION

The Church in France suffered greatly from the religious wars and conflicts of the sixteenth century – abbeys, priories and convents were devastated and many communities barely survived. Yet it was in France that, by the beginning of the seventeenth century, an amazing spiritual renewal was taking place, and this renewal also helped to revitalise Carmel. The first stirrings of Carmelite renewal occurred in the west of France, and this new life was given positive help by the Prior General, Henry Sylvio, who was personally committed to reform in the Order. A revitalised papacy also encouraged renewal so that Rome no longer smothered creative initiatives. However, what mattered most was an openness at the local level to the action of the Spirit.

The renewal of the Order in France owes much to the tact and vision of the Carmelite Philippe Thibault, but the heart of the reform was a blind brother, John of St Samson. Philippe Thibault was a person who respected individuals and had an aversion to excess and legalism. He had a great love of Carmel and wanted to renew the Order by combining the best of its traditions with the vitality of contemporary French movements of spirituality. He was familiar with the Jesuit approach to spirituality and aware of the Discalced Reform that had just been introduced into France. Thibault also sought the support of competent authorities in the Order for his project, and began to work with a combination of vision and realism. He became

Prior of the community at Rennes in July 1608, an event that marks the beginning of the movement in the Order that was to be known as the reform of Touraine. The reform was to revitalise Carmel in France and radically influence the parent body of the Carmelite family worldwide.

However, the soul of the reform was to be John of St Samson or John Moulin. John was born in 1571 at Sens. His family was relatively comfortable, his father being a tax assessor. However, his early years were not idyllic as he caught smallpox when he was three and this led to the loss of his eyesight. His parents died when he was ten, but fortunately his mother's brother took care of him. For many people who lose one sense, another compensates, and John used his acute sense of hearing and love of sound to the full. Music became his enthusiasm, while Ronsard's lyric poetry was his other love. At the age of seventeen he was competent enough to play the organ at St Dominic's in Sens. His love of music and poetry shows a remarkable parallel with the early years of John of the Cross. Beside the organ John played the lute and harp and also wind instruments. He ventured into the realm of composition, writing and arranging a love sonnet for one of his cousins.

In 1597 John left his uncle's home in Sens to be reunited with his brother John Baptist in Paris. John Baptist had spent some years in Italy where he had made his mark and had become part of the Court of Marie de Medici, the future Queen of France. He was married, so a new family, a new household, was there to welcome John. For four years John enjoyed a full and happy life in Paris. He had scope for his music, but also began to develop his prayer life and his devotion to Mary. His brother-in-law, John Douet, proved a good friend, being willing to read to him. However, in 1601 this warm comfortable life came to a sudden end with the death of both John Baptist and his wife Anne. John now depended on people's goodwill and kindness and he gradually sank into near destitution. It was about this time that he began to frequent the Carmelite church at the Place Maubert. In the seventeenth century the Carmelite Priory at Place Maubert was an important centre of studies for the Order in France. Sadly the priory was destroyed during the French Revolution and today only street names give witness to a once vibrant place.

The church at Place Maubert became John's home and he would spend seven or eight hours a day in prayer. To those who saw him he seemed to be peaceful, caught up in divine love. The reality was different – it was a time of darkness and loneliness – but despite the dark John remained faithful.

His material circumstances improved a little when he found a room to live in and also earned some money as organist at the Church of St Pierre aux Boeufs. Gradually John began to build up a relationship with the friars at Place Maubert and also with the people who frequented the church, and in this way he became more confident in talking to people about his prayer life, hoping to learn from others and share his own experiences. It was not easy for him to make contacts as his disability and poverty would have been formidable barriers.

John formed a friendship with a young friar, Matthew Pinault, and through this friendship he drew closer to the Community and was given a room in return for playing and teaching the organ. The next two years were formative and healing for him. He formed around himself a group of friars and lay people and together they began to read spiritual texts. The texts were read aloud and discussed, and John was able to hear both familiar and new material. All this was exciting and it consolidated his own experiences in prayer. At this time he also heard of the ideals of reform that were stirring in the Order, and this inspired him to ask to be admitted to Carmel as a brother.

John received the Carmelite habit at Dol in Brittany. He took the name St Samson at his reception as a novice in 1606, St Samson being a Celtic saint, the first Bishop of Dol. Circumstances at Dol were far from ideal, as the priory was situated in a marshy area, the buildings were ramshackle and the community was poor and not overly observant. Plague ravaged the area over the next few years, and during this time John realised that his prayer had to be translated into practical love and care for the sick – a healing ministry. This healing ministry attracted the attention of Antoine Revol, Bishop of Dol. The Bishop was a man of deep spirituality and he recognised the validity of John's ministry. A friendship was established that was to be of the utmost significance. Antoine Revol was also a friend and disciple of Francis de Sales, but he was willing, in years to come, to see John as his guide in the spiritual life.

In 1612 John moved to the community of Rennes which had now embraced the reform initiated by Philippe Thibault. John was to live at Rennes until his death in 1636. Over these twenty-four years John was the keystone in forming friars in the spirit of the Order. His writings, which he began in 1615, articulate his own vision of prayer, but also lay out the fundamental principles that were to guide the Reform. John's writings come to some four thousand pages of manuscript and, while they were published in the mid-seventeenth century, it is only in the last few years that the critical edition has been attempted. Hein Blommestyn, a Dutch Carmelite of the Titus Brandsma Institute at Nijmegen University, has been entrusted with this important task.

John's life was remarkable, and it is out of that context that his teaching flows. While it is clear there were many authors who influenced him, it was his own personal prayer that inspired his teaching. He had a keen memory, knowing much of the Bible by heart, and he could quote patristic texts with ease. He also knew the Flemish mystics and, while he had no contact with the works of John of the Cross, he knew of Teresa of Avila's writings. His writings also show how deeply he had reflected on the Rule and the *Institute*.

John's Carmelite formation made him emphasise the practice of living in the presence of God like the prophet Elijah, who said, 'The Lord lives in whose presence I stand' (cf. 1 Kings 17:1). Again, like many of his Carmelite predecessors, John believed that all Christians could come to a direct experience of union with God through grace. He was deeply conscious of the generosity of God's love for us, a love that is freely given and utterly transforming. In the face of such overwhelming love the only response is to break out of the shackles of selfishness and allow love to hold us and bring utter fulfilment. At the request of his friend Antoine Revol, the Bishop of Dol, John wrote a treatise, *L'Aiguillon, les flammes, les flèches et le miroir de l'amour de Dieu*, where he tried to outline the way of allowing God's love to shape our lives. This is a book where John takes the reader along paths that he himself has trod. The whole exercise is done with great gentleness and the only thing that John stresses is the need for perseverance. We should conform to the rhythm of Christ's life, putting on Christ's personality, and allow the paschal mystery to energise our lives. We die to self-love to rise into God's gift of love, and move towards new horizons of relationships. John talks of the way we should allow self-love to be purged – and it is at this point that we can submit to God's action. The time of change is difficult and can be challenging, leaving us vulnerable or in darkness. It is at such times we need perseverance. However, when we have let our selfishness be stripped away we are then able to allow the Holy Spirit to breathe through us. This activity of the Spirit – this outpouring of God's love – brings us into a union with the Father as we live in Christ.

The treatise is a good introduction to John's teaching and his way of working with people. He wants us to risk loving God by being close to God, but he sees it as a gentle process that takes us deeper and deeper into the relationship. He uses the image of God's love as being like a wave that laps around life:

> Make use of this very simple aspiration: 'you and I, my love, you and I, you and I, and never another nor more!' To which you could add some burning words like: 'since you are entirely good and all goodness itself; since you are entirely glorious and all glory itself; since you are entirely holy and all holiness itself!'[1]

L'Épithalame, The Wedding Song, is perhaps the most personal and lyrical of John's writings. It is in some respects almost a paraphrase of the Song of Songs and, in its intensity of expression, seems akin to John of the Cross's poetry. This short work in poetic prose expresses the union of John with the eternal wisdom of God. It is an intensely personal expression of total union with God. The experience was so intense that John felt he was dying in the moment of loving embrace with his God. Those who knew John, and especially Donatien of St Nicholas his friend and editor, believed that such intense moments of union took place when John received Communion at Mass. Donatien said that at times John seemed like an angel in human form giving off such a power of love and light. Certainly the language of *The Wedding Song* expresses the ardour of an ecstatic love. There is no clever use of language or rhetoric, only outpourings of love. Love had become an adventure, the whole meaning of John's life.

John's teachings and his way of guiding people had a wide-ranging impact on the Carmelite friars in seventeenth-century France and the sense of renewal gave new life to the whole of the parent branch of the Order. However, Jansenism and Quietism, each in their way did much to discredit mysticism and mystical teaching and as a result John's writings came to be treated with suspicion, or ignored.

John had taught his insights with great sensitivity and gentleness. He did not advocate short cuts to union with God, but emphasised the need for a realistic and disciplined frame-work. The opening up to God could only come through a positive approach to silence and solitude. Time had to be given to the relationship. Again it is important to remember that John experienced deep union during the Eucharist. The time he gave to silence and solitude according to the Rule gave him the focused heart that drew him to the Eucharist and prayer with his community. John was rooted in experience and in the sacraments, and his images of God came from his devotion to the humanity of Christ. Like Teresa of Avila and his Carmelite forebears, the following of Jesus Christ with a pure heart was at the core of his commitment.

LAWRENCE OF THE RESURRECTION

While John of St Samson was forming young friars in Rennes, a young man was growing up in Luneville in Lorraine who was to have a similar impact on young Carmelites. Nicolas Herman was born in 1614 and became a Discalced friar in Paris in 1640. The priory in Rue Vaugirard near the Luxembourg was a fine house of formation for the recently established communities of Discalced friars in France. Nicolas had served as a soldier, but left the army after a bad leg wound. He was accepted as a member of the Paris community as a lay brother and was given the name of Lawrence of the Resurrection.

Lawrence found his first few years in religious life difficult. He felt that compared to the bright young men who were studying theology he himself was rough and awkward. He entered into his work with vigour, spending long hours in the kitchen cooking. During these early years, besides feeling somewhat lost in this large community, Lawrence also experienced a long dark night. His very being was in a state of terrible inner turmoil. He wanted to please God because he was so aware of the beauty and wonder of God, and yet he felt he could never really be good enough to come close to the One he loved. He could only see himself in a negative light. He even reached the stage where he said that he felt that salvation would elude him. Finally, however, he reached a turning point and described what happened in a letter to his spiritual director:

> When I accepted the fact that I might spend my life suffering from these troubles and anxieties – which in no way diminished the trust I had in God and served only to increase my faith – I found myself changed all at once. And my soul, until that time always in turmoil, experienced a deep inner peace as if it had found its centre and place of rest.
>
> Since that time I do my work in simple faith before God, humbly and lovingly, and I carefully apply myself to avoid

doing, saying, or thinking anything that might displease him. I hope that, having done all that I can, he will do with me as he pleases.

I cannot express to you what is taking place in me at present. I feel neither concern nor doubt about my state since I have no will other than the will of God, which I try to carry out in all things and to which I am so surrendered that I would not so much pick up a straw from the ground against his order, nor for any other reason than pure love.

I gave up all devotions and prayers that were not required and I devote myself exclusively to remaining always in his holy presence. I keep myself in his presence by simple attentiveness and a general loving awareness of God that I call 'actual presence of God' or better, a quiet and secret conversation of the soul with God that is lasting. This sometimes results in interior, and often exterior, contentment and joys so great that I have to perform childish acts, appearing more like folly than devotion, to control them and keep them from showing outwardly.

Therefore, Reverend Father, I cannot doubt at all that my soul has been with God for more than thirty years. I will omit a number of things so as not to bore you. I think, however, it would be appropriate to indicate the manner in which I see myself before God, whom I consider as my King.[2]

He had found himself in the presence of God and that state, that reality, became the meaning of his life and the substance of his teaching.

Lawrence spent fifty years in the Carmelite Community in Paris. As he grew older he found work in the kitchen too heavy and he took on the role of sandal-maker. With the passing years more and more people began to see Lawrence as a guide and a friend. He became a great influence on his fellow Carmelites and gradually the word went round that he was a man of insight, holiness and wisdom. Fénèlon, the great Archbishop of Cambrai, came to see him and said he might be rough by nature, but he was delicate in grace.

What we know about Brother Lawrence and the writings attributed to him come through the care and friendship of Joseph de Beaufort. This intelligent but self-effacing priest became a friend of Lawrence in 1666 and was obviously deeply affected by him. De Beaufort ended his life as Vicar-General of the diocese of Paris, respected by Archbishop De Noailles and by the great Fénèlon.

De Beaufort said that Lawrence 'had the best heart in the world'. He was an easy person to be with, warm and understanding. There was nothing inflexible about him, but he had great integrity. He was at home with everyone – with the passage of years his earlier shyness and awkwardness vanished. His long years in Carmel gave him the chance to develop intellectually and he was well versed in the writings of John of the Cross and Teresa, and enjoyed picking the brains of his confrères. As he grew older his leg wound gave him more and more trouble, sciatic pains giving way to severe ulcerations. His last years brought terrible suffering. The last letter he wrote, on 6 February 1691, expresses his hope for peaceful release: 'I hope for the merciful grace of seeing Him in a few days.' He died six days later.

After Lawrence's death De Beaufort gathered his writings, which included some letters and other fragments, and edited them. It is this small collection that is now known as *The Practice of the Presence of God*. Lawrence's writings sadly failed to find favour in France, not for any intrinsic fault, but because he was incorrectly caught up in the Quietist controversy. The fact that Fénèlon admired him became a source of disapproval by association. Quietism was condemned because it taught that perfection was achieved by passivity of the soul before God. In its extreme form Quietism would imply that the will is annihilated and that sin is impossible. In France a great controversy raged over the issue, with Fénèlon sympathetic to the tendency and Bossuet vehemently opposed.

Fénèlon's position was condemned by Pope Innocent XII in 1699, and as a result Brother Lawrence, who stressed abandonment to God's will, was linked to Quietism. Even though any such link was tenuous, Lawrence's work suffered – he was guilty by association. More seriously, however, the reaction against Quietism produced a negative attitude to mysticism which is only receding today. It is interesting that an English translation of Lawrence's writing caught the attention of John Wesley. Wesley was impressed by what he read and included Lawrence in the syllabus of his college at Kingswood, recommending the work to his preachers. For English-speaking Christians Lawrence's work became a classic alongside Thomas à Kempis and Francis de Sales.

Like all Carmelite writers and teachers Lawrence believed that we can come close to God in this life. Union with God is not élitist, it is part of our Christian life. Like John of St Samson, Lawrence appreciated that it is God who loves us first and his love is sheer generous gift. The treasure is offered, and to respond we have only to believe that something beyond our dreams can come into our lives. He wanted people whose lives were pressurised and fragmented to realise that union with God was possible. He saw complicated methods of prayer as a great barrier for most people. Lack of time and the ability to do all that seems necessary can make people feel that prayer is beyond them. He wanted people to realise that we only need to create moments where we allow God to be present to us, to believe that we have an inner life and that there God is happy to dwell. It is a matter of seizing those moments that suddenly become free, even in a busy day, and turning them into time for God. When we are caught in a traffic jam, when the train stops for no reason, we can turn what could be frustration into a moment of grace.

For Lawrence, the more we allow ourselves to be in God's presence, the more change can happen in our lives. Our heart becomes more fixed and focused on God. In the light of God's presence we recognise the changes we need to make and we gain God's perspective in the shaping of our lives. Closeness to God also brings a freedom from negative self-consciousness and this means we feel much more at ease in relating to other people. The fact we know we are lovable to God helps us realise we have something good to share with other people. Being in the presence of God brings a connectedness: everything is brought into right relationship because the love of God becomes the energy that helps us overcome the fears and negativity that so often haunt our lives. All this needs a radical trust that opens us to God and to other people and, crucially, helps us to be much more at ease with ourselves. Certainly, in Lawrence's life, his living in God's presence helped him in his work and his relationships so that he was no longer self-conscious about his roughness or lack of intellectual background. His closeness to God helped him at times when he was entrusted with community business. On a number of occasions he had to oversee the buying and transportation of wine for the community. The journeys to Burgundy and back were physically demanding, but Lawrence learnt to put the project into the context of prayer and, while the responsibility was still great, the business was not allowed to crush his spirit.

Rather than analyse or talk about the core of Lawrence's teaching it would be better to let him speak to us himself:

> On the Presence of God – the [practice of the] presence of God is an application of our mind to God, or a remembrance of God present, that can be brought about either by the imagination or the understanding.
>
> I know someone who, for forty years, has been practising an intellectual presence of God to which he gives several other names. Sometimes he calls it a 'simple act', a 'clear and distinct knowledge of God', an 'indistinct view' or a 'general and loving awareness of God'. Other times he names it 'attention to God', 'silent conversation with God', 'trust in God', or 'the soul's life and peace'. This person told me that all these forms of God's presence are nothing but synonyms for the same thing, and that it is at present second nature to him. Here is how:

This person says that the habit is formed by the rep-
etition of acts and by frequently bringing the mind back
into God's presence. He says that as soon as he is free
from his occupations, and often even when he is most
taken up by them, the recesses of his mind [*esprit*] or the
innermost depths of his soul are raised with no effort on
his part and remain suspended and fixed in God, above
all things, as in its centre and resting place. Since he is
generally aware that his mind, thus held in suspension,
is accompanied by faith, he is satisfied. This is what he
calls 'actual presence of God', which includes all the other
types of presence and much more besides, so that he now
lives as if only he and God were in the world. He converses
with God everywhere, asks him for what he needs, and
rejoices continuously with him in countless ways.

It is important, however, to realize that this conversation with God takes place in the depths and centre of
the soul. It is there that the soul speaks to God heart to
heart, and always in a deep and profound peace that the
soul enjoys in God. Everything that takes place outside
the soul means no more to it than a lit straw that goes
out as soon as it is ignited, and almost never, or very
rarely, disturbs its inner peace.

To get back to the presence of God, I say that this gentle,
loving awareness of God imperceptibly ignites a divine fire
in the soul, inflaming it so intensely with love of God that
one is forced to perform various activities in an effort to
contain it.

We would be surprised to know what the soul sometimes
says to God, who is so pleased with these conversations
that he grants it all its desires, providing it is willing to
remain with him always, and in its centre. To discourage
the soul from returning to created things, God takes care
to provide it with everything it desires, and to such an
extent that it often finds within itself a very savory,
delicious nourishment, though it never sought nor did

anything to obtain it, and in no way contributed to it itself, except by its consent.

The presence of God is then the soul's life and nourishment, which can be acquired by the Lord's grace. Here are the means:

Means to Acquire the Presence of God – the first means is great purity of life.

The second is great fidelity to the practice of this presence and to the fostering of this awareness of God within, which must always be performed gently, humbly, and lovingly, without giving in to disturbance or anxiety.

We must take special care that this inner awareness, no matter how brief it may be, precedes our activities, that it accompanies them from time to time, and that we complete all of them in the same way. Since much time and effort are required to acquire this practice, we must not get discouraged when we fail, for the habit is only formed with effort, yet once it is formed we will find contentment in everything. It is only right that the heart, the first to beat with life and the part that controls the rest of the body, should be the first and the last to love and adore God, whether by beginning or by completing our spiritual and physical activities, and generally in all life's exercises. This is the reason we must take care to foster this awareness, which we must do naturally and normally, as I have said, thus making it easier.

It would be appropriate for beginners to formulate a few words interiorly, such as: 'My God, I am completely yours', or 'God of love, I love you with all my heart', or 'Lord, fashion me according to your heart', or any other words love spontaneously produces. But they must take care that their minds do not wander or return to creatures. The mind must be kept fixed on God alone, so that seeing itself so moved and led by the will, it will be obliged to remain with God.

This [practice of the] presence of God, somewhat difficult in the beginning, secretly accomplishes marvellous effects in the soul, draws abundant graces from the Lord, and, when practised faithfully, imperceptibly leads it to this simple awareness, to this loving view of God present everywhere, which is the holiest, the surest, the easiest, and the most efficacious form of prayer.

Please note that to arrive at this state, mortification of the senses is presupposed, since it is impossible for a soul that still finds some satisfaction in creatures to completely enjoy this divine presence; for to be with God, we must abandon creatures.

Benefits of the Presence of God – the first benefit that the soul receives from the [practice of the] presence of God is that its faith becomes more intense and efficacious in all life's situations, and especially in times of need, since it easily obtains graces in moments of temptation and in the inevitable dealings with creatures. For the soul, accustomed to the practice of faith by this exercise, sees and senses God present by a simple remembrance. It calls out to him easily and effectively, thus obtaining what it needs. It can be said that it possesses here something resembling the state of the blessed, for the more it advances, the more intense its faith grows, becoming so penetrating in the end that you could almost say: I no longer believe, for I see and experience.

The practice of the presence of God strengthens us in hope. Our hope increases in proportion to our knowledge. It grows and is strengthened to the extent that our faith penetrates the secrets of the divinity by this holy exercise, to the extent that it discovers in God a beauty infinitely surpassing not only that of the bodies we see on earth but even that of the most perfect souls and of the angels. The grandeur of the blessing that it desires to enjoy, and in some manner already tastes, satisfies and sustains it.

This practice inspires the will with a scorn for creatures, and inflames it with a sacred fire of love. Since the will is always with God who is a consuming fire, this fire reduces to ashes all that is opposed to it. The soul thus inflamed can live only in the presence of its God, a presence that produces in its heart a holy ardour, a sacred zeal and a strong desire to see this God loved, known, served, and adored by all creatures.

By turning inward and practising the presence of God, the soul becomes so intimate with God that it spends practically all its life in continual acts of love, adoration, contrition, trust, thanksgiving, oblation, petition, and all the most excellent virtues. Sometimes it even becomes one continuous act, because the soul constantly practises this exercise of his divine presence.

I know that few persons reach this advanced state. It is a grace God bestows only on a few chosen souls, since this simple awareness remains ultimately a gift from his kind hand. But let me say, for the consolation of those who desire to embrace this holy practice, that he ordinarily gives it to souls who are disposed to receive it. If he does not give it, we can at least acquire, with the help of ordinary grace, a manner and state of prayer that greatly resembles this simple awareness, by means of this practice of the presence of God.[3]

Much of Lawrence's teaching echoes John of the Cross, but his sense of love, trust and simplicity points forward to Thérèse of Lisieux and to a new context for the Carmelite tradition.

Unlike Thérèse of Lisieux, whose writings and life were to be so readily received by the Church, Lawrence and his fellow seventeenth-century Carmelite John of St Samson fell under the shadow produced by the reaction against Quietism. John and Lawrence shaped the lives of their contemporaries both in Carmel and in society at large, but by the end of the seventeenth century their works had been sidelined. However, today their voices are again being heard and they can be seen as belonging firmly within the long tradition of Carmelite spirituality. Certainly both speak clearly as Carmelites of the call of all people to a closeness to God in this life.

7. LOVE IN THE HEART OF THE CHURCH – THÉRÈSE OF LISIEUX

Thérèse Martin, often known as the Little Flower, has recently been declared a Doctor of the Church. This ranks her along with such figures as Augustine, Thomas Aquinas and Teresa of Avila. Thérèse was not a great writer like Augustine, but she did something crucial: she helped to bring spirituality and theology together again, demonstrating in word and by her life the centrality of prayer and love for theology. She is an important impetus in the Church's rediscovery of the value of the mystical and its moving away from the over-intellectual approach to theology that had been fostered since the seventeenth century. The reaction to Quietism was at last being addressed.

Thérèse had to transcend many aspects of life both in society and in the Church, and even after death her true self was almost submerged. She was born in Normandy in 1873 into a devout Roman Catholic family, at a time when Roman Catholicism in France was very much on the defensive. Catholics saw themselves as under siege in a rationalist, anti-clerical world. In their retreat to a 'fortress Church' Catholics brought with them an often pietistic faith. There was a retreat into piety and devotion, a withdrawal into a safe space – almost a private world. Allied to a disapproval of secular society and a nostalgia for the *ancien régime*, such Catholics adopted a fierce middle-class respectability. 'What will people think?' was often the criterion of behaviour. These attitudes coloured Thérèse's family life and were certainly present in community life in Carmel where she spent the last nine years of her life. It was this spirit of correctness that caused Thérèse's sister to edit her manuscript so that the early editions of *The Story of a Soul* contained radical revisions. Since the 1950s the original manuscripts have been available, and also original photographs that show a more vigorous person, a real human being.

The remarkable aspect of Thérèse's life and ministry was the way she was able to live her years in Carmel with such maturity and creativity. She was the author of her own vision of life and there is a genuine originality in what she wrote and how she lived. Thérèse was a Carmelite in her faithful following of Jesus: he was her guide. Sadly she was not able to immerse herself in the Scriptures after the spirit of the Rule, because the Bible was not readily available in the French Church of that time. Bourgeois susceptibility led to the attitude that many passages of Scripture were too realistic, not 'nice'. The realities of human nature were too much for the post-Jansenist mind. Despite these difficulties, Thérèse was able to read the New Testament and she eventually obtained a Bible.

When Teresa of Avila founded her Carmels she wanted them to be communities where friendship could flourish and a simple lifestyle could be realised. She did not want communities to be too large because institutionalism could creep in and financial problems could grow. The Carmel at Lisieux was not entirely in that mould. The community numbered about twenty-five, and it is clear some of the nuns were difficult characters. The Prioress, Mother Gonzaga, came from the nobility and never freed herself from her background. There was tension between her and Thérèse's sisters, and sometimes the community had to wait on the Prioress's visiting relatives. The Rule was interpreted with a strictness that missed its essential humanity and was certainly far from Teresa of Avila's creative spirit. Mother Gonzaga was strict in her vision of Carmelite life both for others and for herself. This rage for correctness and the entrenched bourgeois mentality touched Thérèse during her illness when the community went into denial over its nature. For whatever reason, tuberculosis was seen as a disease to be ashamed of – it was an attitude not unlike that adopted today by some people to HIV/AIDS.

The great achievement is that Thérèse emerges from this unlikely environment to be so original, creative and self-possessed. She achieved an autonomy that is remarkable, and she was a likeable, strong-minded, humorous and idealistic young woman. She could have been dependent on her sisters, she could have played the games others played, but she found her own place in which to be.

Thérèse always had a lively imagination and a sense of fun. This aspect of her personality enabled her to feel free as a writer, expressive as a poet and fascinated by theatre. She had a great admiration for Joan of Arc, admiring her courage and decisiveness, and there is a striking photograph of her playing the part of the Maid of Orleans in a dramatic presentation she organised for the community. This lively imagination links her to the great sixteenth-century Carmelites, Teresa of Avila and John of the Cross. Thérèse shared the great Teresa's romanticism and clear vision. She also lived out in her last months the passive night of the spirit that John of the Cross spoke about in his commentaries. Thérèse knew the writings of the Carmelite Spanish mystics and her teaching on love echoes and repeats John's own words in a new and creative way.

Thérèse stands at the centre of the Carmelite tradition with her belief that we can all achieve closeness to God through our prayer and our following of Jesus Christ as we live the Gospel. This is her teaching on the 'Little Way'. For Thérèse, holiness, closeness to God, is not achieved by spectacular ascetic practices. We come to God by infusing love into every aspect of life. The 'Little Way' is one of childlike trust in God, but it is not infantile and naive, or a searching for the lost innocence of some idealised childhood. Thérèse had known through childhood and early adolescence the pain of separation from those she loved. However, she gained the maturity to realise that trust and consistency were possible, and she began to express them in her wholehearted commitment to God. She wanted a quiet hidden relationship, to live out in secret her love for

God. This 'Little Way' was a reaction to the strictness and spectacular ascetic practices that seemed to be demanded by her Prioress.

Thérèse was able to come to God in such loving trust because, like Teresa of Avila, she realised that the humanity of Christ was at the heart of Christianity. Jesus is the source of love and happiness for her – the Gospels were her book.

However, the most profound insights of Thérèse came during the last eighteen months of her life. Her illness took hold with full seriousness at Easter 1896 and became progressively more painful and crippling. During these last months of her life Thérèse underwent the passive night of the spirit. For her, the experience was one that seemed like the purification of purgatory. She felt she had been placed in darkness and that her belief was an illusion. She began to feel that heaven could not exist. It was as if she had been placed in solidarity with non-believers. This struggle was to last until her death. Most difficult of all were the times when she found not just blasphemous thoughts but even blasphemous words welling up inside her. Mocking voices spoke to her, telling her that in the end there was just nothing – it was all an illusion. Thérèse even began to think that science would be able to disprove everything and end up explaining God's existence away. She felt the force of rationalism like a great wave ready to sweep away all traces of belief and, in her own way, she was akin to Matthew Arnold and the grey vision of 'Dover Beach'. Even more terrifying for her were suicidal thoughts of ending the pain and the sense of futility:

> Watch carefully, Mother, when you will have patients a prey to violent pains; don't leave them any medicines that are poisonous. I assure you, it needs only a second when one suffers intensely to lose one's reason. Then one would easily poison oneself.

However, just before her death she was able to say,

> Yes! What a grace it is to have faith. If I had not had

faith, I would have committed suicide without an instant's hesitation.[1]

In his insightful study on Thérèse, *Love in the Heart of the Church*, Chris O'Donnell has shown that Thérèse's experiences have something important to teach us about terminal illness, and may help people face death in an age when there is so much denial about its reality. The doubts and the trial do pass, and in Thérèse's writing we are helped to understand that even in the dark we are not abandoned by God. She is a living commentary on John of the Cross's teaching.

During this time of trial and struggle Thérèse clung on to her relationship with God and tried to express her love in her poems and in her relationships with the community. It was only when she was very near to death that those closest to her became aware of her struggle, and even then perhaps could only guess at what was happening.

In the October of 1896 in the middle of her sufferings Thérèse had a moment of light and insight which helped her to find a sense of what her life was really about and what her real vocation was. Perhaps it is best to allow her to describe the moment and its import in her own words:

> My desires caused me a veritable martyrdom, and I opened the Epistles of St Paul to find some kind of answer. Chapters Twelve and Thirteen of the First Epistle to the Corinthians fell under my eyes. I read there, in the first of these chapters, that all cannot be apostles, prophets, doctors, and so on, that the Church is composed of different members, and that the eye cannot be the hand at one and the same time. The answer was clear, but it did not fulfil my desires and gave me no peace. Without becoming discouraged, I continued my reading, and this sentence consoled me: 'Yet strive for the better gifts, and I point out to you a yet more excellent way.' And the Apostle explains how all the most perfect gifts are nothing without love. That charity is the excellent way that leads most surely to God.

I finally had to rest. Considering the mystical body of the Church, I had not recognized myself in any of the members described by St Paul, or rather I desired to see myself in them all. Charity gave me the key to my vocation. I understood that if the Church had a body composed of different members, the most necessary and most noble of all could not be lacking to it, and so I understood that the Church had a heart and that this heart was burning with love. I understood it was love alone that made the Church's members act, that if love ever became extinct, apostles would not preach the Gospel and martyrs would not shed their blood. I understood that love comprised all vocations, that love was everything, that it embraced all times and places ... in a word, that it was eternal!

Then, in the excess of my delirious joy, I cried out: 'O Jesus, my Love ... my vocation, at last I have found it ... my vocation is Love!'

Yes I have found my place in the Church and it is you, O my God, who have given me this place: in the heart of the Church, my mother, I shall be love. Thus I shall be everything, and thus my dream will be realized.[2]

Thérèse found her vocation in love – love at the heart of the Church. She came to this insight as she read St Paul's letters and discovered his teaching on the Mystical Body. This Pauline vision with its emphasis on the Spirit gave Thérèse a generous sense of the Church which helped her to see herself as a missionary even though she never left Carmel. It also enhanced her awareness of the Communion of Saints. This profound awareness of the Church is akin to Teresa of Avila's missionary sense when, in the context of the Reformation, she sought a healing mission in the Church.

One of the rich veins of spirituality that flow from the doctrine of the Communion of Saints is a wonderful appreciation of intercessory prayer. The notion of belonging to a fellowship that goes beyond the here and now is also a powerful antidote to an individualistic approach to salvation.

For Thérèse the saints were her friends. This sense of intimacy began with her attraction to the life of Joan of Arc, but soon extended to other saints and especially to Mary, the Mother of Jesus. She also had a belief that members of her family who had died were part of that community of love and that in a special way a closeness was achieved in the Eucharist between those in heaven and those on earth. Her Church, her community, was one that went beyond the limits of time and space. She spoke to the saints as friends and asked them to intercede for those troubled by doubt or experiencing loss of faith.

Her sense of love being the energy of the Church was the inspiration for her missionary dreams and her support for priests. She had hopes that she might be sent to the Carmel that was being set up in Saigon. However, realising that her health was broken, she turned her energies into a power of love for all involved in that work. She hoped that her prayers, her pain, could support those working to bring the Gospel to remote areas of the world. Once again it was her deep reflection on Paul's teaching that helped her live out the doctrine of the Mystical Body.

Thérèse had a great love for priests and their ministry. It is possible to read her works with our modern eyes and to wonder if she ever wanted to be a priest herself. Certainly her deep sense of communion with Jesus in the Eucharist made her value the liturgy above all else, and she saw the role of those who ministered at the altar as precious. In the last months of her life she was involved in correspondence with two missionary priests. Her enthusiasm and commitment in offering them support and encouragement is amazing given her frail health and the darkness of spirit she was enduring. Her words are full of energy and her warmth of understanding shows her generosity and altruism. She maintained the correspondence almost to the end of her life, and in a poem to Father Roulland, who was ministering in China, she writes:

Heaven for me is feeling within myself the resemblance
Of the God who created me with his Powerful Breath.
Heaven for me is remaining always in his presence,
Calling him my Father and being his child.
In his Divine arms, I don't fear the storm.
Total abandonment is my only law.
Sleeping on his Heart, right next to his Face,
    That is Heaven for me! . . .

I've found my Heaven in the Blessed Trinity
That dwells in my heart, my prisoner of love.
There, contemplating my God, I fearlessly tell him
That I want to serve him and love him forever.
Heaven for me is smiling at this God whom I adore
When He wants to hide to try my faith.
To suffer while waiting for him to look at me again
    That is Heaven for me! . . .[3]

Thérèse's greatness is her ability to grasp that the Christian
life is the realisation of love in the community where you live.
Moreover, that community, if inspired by the dynamic of love,
will always be open and creative. She realised that the call to
love was linked to the same obedience that brought Jesus
to the Cross. Her last months were a painful journey to Jerusalem and to her Calvary. Like Jesus she came to the end in
a time of terrible darkness and in this she fulfilled her faithful
following, her allegiance to him. By faith she grasped the
meaning of the heavenly Jerusalem. Yet at times during her
last months she felt as if that reality could be snatched away
from her, that her hope might even be in vain. We know that
she kept journeying and in the end peace broke through the
darkness and the pain.

However, the great contribution, the message that Thérèse
has for us today, is of the self-sacrificing love that Christ has
for his community. By her life Thérèse became an icon of that
love and shows us a face of the Church that is more than
the institution. The writer Chris O'Donnell is influenced by the
theology of von Balthasar when he says that Thérèse has

something vital to teach the post-Vatican II Church. If we want a renewed and missionary Church we need to move away from mere organisational and structural change and live love. We will then see the wonderful reality of the Communion of Saints and learn to understand how much worth there is in an act of pure love – in living the 'Little Way'. In her discipleship Thérèse is in many ways a wonderful window into the faith of Mary, whose unconditional trust lived through Calvary and then experienced the fullness of the Resurrection.

The Letter to the Ephesians speaks of all of us as 'God's work of art'. Thérèse is an immortal diamond, crafted by love in her suffering and in her creative way of living life. She was strongly inserted in the Carmelite tradition, living the Rule, and loving the Scriptures. Like Elijah, she too journeyed to her own meeting with God. Like the prophet, she came to the end of her tether, yet was fed and enabled to carry on. The prophet encountered God in the Wadi Cherith and on Horeb. Thérèse journeyed with Christ and came to the eternal Mount Sion and the New Jerusalem.

8. TRUTH AND PROPHECY – EDITH STEIN AND TITUS BRANDSMA

The twentieth century can seem like the most paradoxical of times. The boundaries of knowledge have expanded beyond our dreams, disease and hunger can be conquered, and yet we have teetered on the brink of extermination. The century has seen the Declaration of Human Rights and also genocide. In this turbulent period the Carmelite family has found a renewed vigour and some of the damage generated in the sixteenth century within the family has found healing. Two Carmelites, Titus Brandsma and Edith Stein, stand out in the twentieth century and their lives express in this troubled context the key elements of the Carmelite tradition.

Titus Brandsma was born in Friesland in the Netherlands in 1881, and died in Dachau in 1942. Categorised by the Nazis as a 'dangerous little friar', to his brothers Titus was a man of prayer and an exponent of the deepest values. He was never physically strong, but he had an enormous capacity for work and a passion for the truth. Titus became a Carmelite in 1898, happy though still a teenager to embrace silence and solitude. These basic values of the Rule were with him even in his busiest days and certainly in his last days in Nazi prisons.

The Carmelite friars had suffered in the upheavals that began with the French Revolution and continued under the anti-clerical laws enacted throughout Europe in the nineteenth century. However, the Netherlands had not joined in the process of attacking religious life and Dutch Carmelites were at the forefront of rebuilding the Order. It was in this context that Titus received his initial formation as a friar.

After studies in Rome, Titus returned to his homeland to

teach philosophy, and in 1923 he helped found the Catholic University of Nijmegen. He gave unsparingly of his time and energy to the university, eventually becoming the Rector Magnificus. Involvement in university life has never been unusual for Carmelites down through the Middle Ages and to the present day. This involvement has been an important aspect of the Order's tradition. For Titus, university life was not purely academic, but included a loving care for his students. He was always ready to listen, advise and be an advocate. Besides teaching philosophy Titus was also interested in mysticism. He had a great love for the mystics of the Low Countries and also for his famous Carmelite fore- bears. In his desire to spread awareness of the mystics he travelled widely and was not afraid to speak on a popular non- academic level. In 1935 he spent time in Ireland and North America lecturing, and in the course of a lecture in Washington he spoke of the apostolate of the contemplative life:

> But the principal point to remember is that the school of Carmel, while rating at its highest the cure of souls in the world, cannot forget that it is called to a higher vocation. Elias was called to a life of prayer in the midst of a life of intense activity, yet he is one of the greatest Prophets of the Old Testament. His life and prayer tell us that his prayer was the strength of his life. So the contemplative prayer of the Carmelite is also the strength of the active apostolate. The influence of the contemplative soul is not withheld from the apostolate. In the mystical Body of Christ – we shall see that more clearly in the last lecture – the prayers and sacrifices of the contemplatives repre- sent an organ of high value. So there is no opposition of the contemplative life to the active. The former is the great support of the latter. The mystical life is in the highest sense apostolic. Without activity it has the greatest influ- ence. St Teresa of Avila, St Mary Magdalen de Pazzi and especially the little St Thérèse of Lisieux teach us the apostolate of prayer. Many Carmels are considered the real

centres of missionary work, not because of their activity
but because of their contemplative life.[1]

Titus believed in the seamlessness of the Christian life –
prayer and work were parts of the whole. Whenever he was
called from silence and solitude to help someone he would say
he was leaving God for God.

In 1935 he became chaplain to Dutch Catholic journalists
and it was this role in the context of the rise of Nazi power
that was to lead to his calvary at Dachau. Titus not only
advised the journalists on matters of faith, but fought to get
better working conditions and championed the aspirations of
their trade union. He was proud in his turn to belong to the
Dutch N.U.J. However, back in his university context Titus
began to attack the lies behind Nazi ideology, particularly its
neopaganism and racism. In a letter to the President of the
Theology Faculty at Nijmegen University he outlined his
strategy:

> Distinguished Colleague,
> In reply to your appreciated letter of November 30, I will
> give you my opinion: the Catholic faith in our country is
> seriously threatened and weakened by very many doc-
> trines which culminate in German National Socialism, in
> which they find their strongest expression. These doc-
> trines are attractive. This influence can best be halted
> on the one hand by exposing the theory of this National
> Socialism and the philosophy from which it rose – above
> all that of Nietzsche – in its lamentable tendencies, and
> to confute it. On the other hand by clearly stressing, in
> an enthusiastic and positive way, the value of the human
> person in both the natural and supernatural orders.
>
> In reply to the question what have we done in a practical
> way, I think it is sufficient to note that during the past
> academic year, in my university course on the history
> of contemporary philosophy, I gave lessons on National
> Socialism from a philosophical viewpoint, and in my
> course on the Philosophy of History I spoke for the whole

year about the growth and development of National Socialism as a typical example of a reactionary phenomenon.

I am always willing to provide further information.

Yours in Christ

Father Titus Brandsma O. Carm[2]

After the invasion of the Netherlands in 1940 Titus continued his work with journalists. Then in collaboration with Archbishop de Jong he began to stiffen the resolve of the Roman Catholic press to ensure that they would not collaborate with the Nazi propaganda machine. In late 1941 and early 1942 Titus criss-crossed the country, urging editors and proprietors to stand firm and not to accept advertising or handouts from the Nazis. It seems that his work was betrayed to the authorities and in January 1942 he was arrested. By now he was over sixty years old and his health, which had never been robust, was becoming frail. A period of interrogation and imprisonment began a time that Titus turned into an experience of contemplative solitude. This period of imprisonment in some ways mirrors the suffering of his great mentor John of the Cross.

Titus was imprisoned first of all at Scheveningen, a police prison, and while any prison regime is harsh, he found peace and solitude in his enforced isolation. He found himself repeating time and again Teresa's prayer, 'Let nothing disturb thee, let nothing frighten thee. All things are passing, God does not change. Whoever possesses God wants for nothing. God alone suffices.'

Writing about his cell on 27 January 1942, Titus said:

> 'Beata solitudo, blessed solitude.' I am already quite at home in this small cell. I have not yet got bored here, just the contrary. I am alone, certainly, but never was Our Lord so near to me. I could shout for joy because he made me find him again entirely, without me being able to go to see people, nor people me. Now he is my only refuge, and I

feel secure and happy. I would stay here for ever, if he so disposed. Seldom have I been so happy and content.
Scheveningen, January 27, 1942.[3]

In Scheveningen, while meditating on the humanity of Christ, Titus composed a poem that is particularly precious to those who have come to know his life:

O Jesus when I look on you
My love for you starts up anew,
And tells me that your heart loves me
and you my special friend would be.

> More courage I will need for sure,
> But any pain I will endure,
> Because it makes me like to you
> And leads unto your kingdom too.

In sorrow do I find my bliss,
For sorrow now no more is this:
Rather the path that must be trod,
That makes me one with you, my God.

> Oh, leave me here alone and still,
> And all around the cold and chill.
> To enter here I will have none;
> I weary not when I'm alone.

For, Jesus, you are at my side;
Never so close did we abide.
Stay with me, Jesus, my delight,
Your presence near makes all things right.[4]

In the spring of 1942, Titus was moved to Amersfoort. This was a transit camp holding 800 prisoners drawn from all walks of Dutch life – resistance fighters, intelligentsia and clergy. Conditions were severe, dysentery was rife and all the prisoners were forced to wear stark uniforms. Titus began a ministry to his fellow prisoners and, despite being ill, tried to comfort those around him and to hear confessions. On Good

Friday evening he was asked to give a lecture and he spoke about mysticism, about experiencing God and being aware of God suffering in Jesus Christ. An eyewitness recalls how Titus seemed transfigured as he spoke and touched each person present as they struggled with their misery. He gave them a key, and that key was the love of God.

Titus was transferred to Dachau where his health deteriorated quickly. The last part of his living out of Christ's Passion was relatively brief and he was soon taken to the prison hospital. Shortly after 16 July, the Feast of Our Lady of Mount Carmel, on a cold rainy morning he was beaten up by the guards. A fellow Carmelite, Brother Raphael, who was also a prisoner, took him to the hospital. For a few days as he lay there, exhausted and weak, doctors experimented on him until a nurse gave him a fatal injection at 2.00 p.m. on 26 July. Titus's last act was to try and help the nurse – bring her back to love and to God. His final act was an attempt to mediate love. We do know that this encounter was to bring this woman back to God, as years later she visited a Carmelite community seeking reconciliation.

Titus walked his lonely road conscious of his call to follow Christ, but conscious like Thérèse of the need to live out love in the Church. He stood for truth, rejected anti-Semitism and dreamt of reconciliation. Even during his interrogation he professed his love for the German people and looked to the day when peace and friendship would be re-established. At the time of Titus's death the clouds grew darker and the Nazis took reprisals by singling out Roman Catholics of Jewish origin to make the point that they would brook no opposition. In his life Titus constantly opened up the springs of God's love, but tragically in Europe the cancer of anti-Semitism created a culture of death. It seemed that the prophetic voice was silenced, but the light can never be finally overcome by the dark.

Titus offered a prophetic voice at a time when gospel values were under attack. Like Elijah, he was called to face and challenge the establishment. I believe he was conscious that his calling had to include this social-prophetic dimension. Like any prophet he saw that the creative tradition flowing from the Scriptures was undermined by an ideology that contradicted the message of light and life. Because Titus was a philosopher, he recognised the fallacy of Nazi ideology, but because he was a Carmelite he knew he had to take a stand that would help other people of faith to resist. His final journey, like Elijah's, was to a meeting with God, and this was also to be his full entry into the Easter mystery. He was purified and brought to union with God through the systematic cruelty of the concentration camp, and yet he was able to touch springs of faith that helped him reach beyond the dark. In this last journey he was open to others, confirming their faith by his ministry of word and sacrament.

Shortly after Titus Brandsma's death in Dachau, Edith Stein, the philosopher and Carmelite nun, was arrested and within days died in Auschwitz. Edith was arrested because, though a Roman Catholic, she was Jewish by birth, and the Nazis were attacking the Catholic Church because the Dutch bishops, inspired by Titus, had spoken out against anti-Semitism. Edith Stein, like Titus, was passionate for the truth. In her prayer she came to embrace the Cross as she identified with the humanity of Christ.

Edith was born in Breslau, Germany, in 1891, the youngest of the eleven children of a devout Jewish family. Her family were hard-working business people, but tragedy struck when Edith was only two, with the unexpected death of her father. Fortunately Edith's mother, a gifted and energetic person, was able to care for her children. Auguste was never afraid of hard work and she had great trust in God.

Edith proved to be a precocious child and was somewhat turbulent as she entered her teens. From the age of thirteen to twenty-one she did not believe in God. At one stage she gave up school, but after a year she resumed her education and began to discover philosophy. By the age of twenty philosophy was at the heart of her life and at Göttingen University she discovered Husserl and phenomenology. For Edith, Husserl was the master, and after finishing her doctorate on 'Empathy' she worked as his assistant. Friends found Edith passionate for the truth, interested in women's rights, but above all a warm human being generous and hospitable. She was an attractive personality, made more so by her warm-heartedness. An extract from *Life in a Jewish Family* shows her emerging vision of life, especially her passionate commitment to women's rights:

> My love for history was not a romantic escape from the past. It was closely bound up with a passionate involvement in present-day politics – in history in the making. Both of these interests stemmed from an unusually strong sense of social responsibility on my part – a feeling for the solidarity of mankind and also of its smaller communities. Repellent as Darwinian nationalism was to me, I had always been convinced of the significance and inborn historical necessity of having individual states with peoples and nations of distinct character. This was the reason socialist ideologies and international movements had never been able to gain any hold on me. As time went on, I found myself gradually moving away from the liberal notions I had grown up with, and moving towards a more positive concept of the state, one which resembled conservatism but without a specific commitment to its Prussian form.[5]

During this period in Göttingen Edith began to change. The philosophers she worked with were willing to debate religious issues, and so she was opened up to both Jewish and Christian thinking. It was also a time when she dreamt of an academic career and marriage.

About this time she began to struggle with the God question. She described the devices she used to keep God at bay:

> A convinced atheist learns through personal experience that there actually is a God. Now faith can no longer be eluded. Yet he can still refuse to ground himself in it or

to let it become effective in him, choosing instead to hold on to the 'scientific worldview' that he knows an unmitigated faith would be the end of ... Or again, someone can offer me affection. There's no way I can stop him from doing it, but I don't have to respond to it. I can always pull myself away.[6]

However, it was perhaps in day-to-day life that Edith began to feel drawn to belief. A chance visit to the cathedral proved to be an eye-opener:

We went into the cathedral for a few moments, and as we stood there in respectful silence, a woman came in with her shopping basket and knelt down in one of the pews to say a short prayer. That was something completely new to me. In the synagogue, as in the Protestant churches I had visited, people only went in at the time of the service. But here was someone coming into the empty church in the middle of a day's work as if to talk with a friend. I have never been able to forget that.[7]

Edith began reading the Gospels and also Kierkegaard. She found the Danish philosopher daunting in his vision of the individual and God. The turning point for Edith came when she was staying with friends and she picked up Teresa of Avila's *Life*. Here Edith found a God of love. She also felt a kinship with Teresa, finding herself at home with Teresa's honesty and directness. At last she had found a place where she could be at peace. In January 1922 Edith was baptised. Her mother wept at the news, but tried to understand what God was doing in her daughter. For Edith, her conversion also revitalised her Jewish roots and over the years she was assiduous in attending the synagogue whenever she was at home.

Edith's conversion came at a time when she realised that an academic career was not open to her. Women were passed over when university posts became available, so she began to teach at the Dominican school at Speyer. For eleven years she taught, lectured, studied and prayed. Her life was immensely full and her intellectual horizons were constantly widening. She discovered the writings of Cardinal Newman and began to translate some of the works of Thomas Aquinas. She now saw her scholarship as a way of serving God. More important for her was her discovery that Thomas Aquinas the philosopher was one who saw the primacy of love in God, and that there was a way of loving knowledge that could lead to union with God. Like Teresa of Avila, Thomas was a mystic who realised that the wisdom infused within us by God could make all else seem like straw.

Edith found a home at Beuron Abbey, where she would spend the great feasts of the Church in prayer. When one night she was locked in the Abbey church she saw 'the vigil' as a special gift.

During the period from 1922 to 1933 Edith was concerned with developing her ideas on the role of women in contemporary society. Some of her lectures are now available in English in the second volume of her *Collected Works*. She wanted to develop a more adequate concept of the human person so that women could be shown to have a unique inalienable value of their own. Edith wanted women to have access to the professions in such a way as to enhance the professions without women being fragmented by conflicting demands. She was eager to reform the education system to make it more holistic so that women could develop their potential. In many ways she was like Teilhard de Chardin, pointing out that certain qualities that can be labelled male are no longer appropriate for complex societies that need a greater capacity for understanding and imagination.

Edith also became aware of the creeping influence of Nazi ideology on the role of women, and of some of the negative attitudes in Marxism:

> Curiously, this romantic view is connected to that brutal attitude which considers woman merely from the biological point of view; indeed, this is the attitude which

characterizes the political group now in power. Gains won during the last decades are being wiped out because of this romanticist ideology, the use of women to bear babies of Aryan stock, and the present economic situation. The woman is being confined to housework and to family. In doing so, the spiritual nature of woman is as little considered as the principles of her historical development. Not only is violence being done to the spirit by a biological misinterpretation and by today's economic trends but, also, by the materialistic and fundamental point of view of opposing groups.

Through the bait of radical equalization with men, the feminine following can also be recruited by a politics which views woman as an important factor not only in economics but in the class struggle. But the callous disregard of woman's nature and destiny is running into very strong opposition, especially among young women.[8]

By 1933 Edith was determined to enter Carmel. In the decade since her conversion she had followed Jesus through her focused prayer life, and in her work for women had shown a courage akin to that of the great Teresa. Now another reality emerged that was to make her express herself in a prophetic way – National Socialism and its anti-Semitic thrust. Edith became aware that Hitler's rise to power heralded persecution of the Jewish people. She was a patriotic German, but proud of her Jewish heritage. Now she saw a climate where it was permissible to attack Jews and their property. Under the new order she lost her job in Münster because she was Jewish. She recognised the real danger to the Jewish people and tried to gain an audience with Pope Pius XI to help him understand what was fermenting in Germany. Her request was refused and her subsequent appeal to the Pope that he should condemn Nazi racism in an encyclical received no response.

Edith saw this as the time to enter Carmel, so that in closer union with Jesus Christ she could carry the cross that was now being laid on the Jewish people. Her family saw her entry into Carmel as almost a desertion of her people who were undergoing persecution. Her mother, now aged 84, was inconsolable. No explanation could satisfy her and Edith found this time 'a step that had to be taken in the absolute darkness of faith'.

Edith entered the Cologne Carmel in October 1933. It was a move from being Fräulein Doktor, lecturer and educationalist, to being a postulant, the newest member of the community. The Cologne Carmel proved a congenial community for Edith. While she had to get used to routine and humdrum tasks, her superiors respected her and allowed her to continue with her writing. The years at Cologne were a time of deep growth and freedom, but always set against the growing darkness of the Nazi regime.

During her early years in Cologne, Edith worked on a philosophical treatise, *Finite and Eternal Being*. In this work she brought together her insights from phenomenological philosophy and from her study of Thomas Aquinas. She was fascinated by the structure of the human person, and made her research into personal being the basis of her attempt to comprehend the nature of all created reality. For Edith the individual person incarnates a unique spiritual value, and that spiritual value comes from the way we image God. She relished the sense of objectivity that phenomenology opened up, but she also wanted to explore concepts of transcendence. She wanted to move from considering things as they appear to seeing them in the ground of their being, in their essence. This movement was for her an opening on to the reality of God, the source of all being and of all persons. She saw the human person as a complex unity of body, mind and spirit. Because the human person was spirit it could reach beyond itself and relate to other persons and also transcend the objects of immediate experience. As she tried to synthesise phenomenology and Thomism, Edith was bound to disappoint those thinkers who eschewed metaphysics, but her openness to the transcendent came from her prayer life, her relationship with God and with her neighbour. She could no longer see philo-

sophy as a purely intellectual exercise. Her awareness of the
openness of the human person to 'the other', to a sense of
community, and her embrace of transcendence all came from
her prayer. She understood that it was during prayer that the
soul discovers itself and realises that its goal is union with
the Creator. Her study of Thomas made her realise that he
was primarily a theologian and a mystic for whom philosophy
assisted the process of understanding all that arose from the
experience of faith.

This philosophical research was not published, because by
1936 the Nazis would not allow publications by non-Aryans.
At the same time Edith was growing in her mystical awareness. Even before she entered Carmel she was aware of the
need to follow Christ with an undivided heart: 'Only by following Christ is it possible to hold on to him.' She admired
the way Teresa of Avila had been drawn more deeply into the
'Interior Castle' where the Lord could speak to her. Teresa was
faithful to Elijah's spirit, aflame with zeal for the God of hosts.
For Edith Teresa represents the mystical current at the heart
of the Church's life of prayer. This current is essential for the
very existence of the Church, but sadly for a long time this
realisation was absent from its life and practice.

In *Finite and Eternal Being* she states categorically:

The mystic is simply a person who has an experiential
knowledge of the teaching of the Church: that God dwells
in the soul. Anyone who feels inspired by this dogma to
search for God will end up taking the same route the
mystic is led along: he will retreat from the realm of
the senses, the images of the memory and the natural
functioning of the intellect, and will withdraw into the
barren solitude of the inner self, to dwell in the darkness
of faith through a simple loving glance of the Spirit of
God, who is present although concealed. There he will
remain in profound peace, as in 'the place of rest', until
the Lord decides to transform his faith into vision.[9]

With this sort of language Edith is, like Thérèse of Lisieux, trying to reunite spirituality and the life of the Church.

For Edith every true prayer is a prayer of the Church. A poem she wrote at Pentecost 1942 shows, in the spirit of John of the Cross, how the Holy Spirit enables that prayer life:

> Who are You, sweet light that fills me
> And illumines the darkness of my heart?
> You guide me like a mother's hand,
> And if You let me go, I could not take
> Another step.
> You are the space
> That surrounds and contains my being.
> Without You it would sink into the abyss
> Of nothingness from which You raised it into being.
> You, closer to me than I to myself,
> More inward than my innermost being –
> And yet unreachable, untouchable,
> And bursting the confines of any name:
> > Holy Spirit –
> > > Eternal love![10]

In 1936 Edith's mother died. Mother and daughter were never fully reconciled, but communication had been resumed. Frau Stein died before the savage onslaught against the Jewish people began. That persecution was signalled by the events of 8 November 1938, the 'Kristallnacht', when Jewish property and synagogues were destroyed. Many Jews tried to flee the country and some of Edith's family did get to America. However, her sisters Rosa and Frieda and her brother Paul were not allowed to leave. Edith began to realise that perhaps she was going to die; perhaps, like Esther, she could intercede for her people. On New Year's Eve she left Cologne and was driven across the border to join the community at Echt in the Netherlands. Her superiors felt that she would be safer outside the confines of the Third Reich.

Edith soon settled into life in her new community. The Carmel at Echt was somewhat more conservative than

Cologne, but Edith was allowed to continue her writing. At one stage the Prioress suggested that Edith should use a book to help her fight the sleep that attacked her during meditation. Edith tried to get the Prioress to understand that her prayer came from her heart and that the sleep came from her inability to rest well at night.

During this period she began to immerse herself more and more in the Easter mystery. She began to see the mystery of the Cross and suffering as the very energy of her life in Christ. She saw Jesus as the one who was able to live the dark night to the full. She reflected on the Passion, focusing on the way Jesus lived out the prophecies of the suffering servant as expressed in Isaiah: 'A man despised and familiar with sorrow'. She also understood the sense of abandonment that Jesus experienced on the cross that led to his terrible cry: 'My God, my God, why hast Thou forsaken me?'

Many years before, in January 1931, Edith had given a lecture at Ludwigshafen. She spoke of the mystery of Christmas and of seeing the child as the Redeemer. The love that draws us to the manger draws us to follow Jesus along the way of the Cross:

> Whoever belongs to Christ must go the whole way with him. They must mature and become adult, they must one day or other walk the way of the cross to Gethsemane and Golgotha. And all external sufferings are as nothing compared with the dark night of the soul, when the divine light no longer shines and the voice of the Lord no longer speaks. God is there, but hidden and silent.[11]

In all this Edith speaks of trust in God – we will feel God's guiding hand. Again she says,

> Even in the dark night of personal distance from God and abandonment the one who is allied to God will stick it out firm as a rock ... Thy will be done even in the darkest night ... 'The road of the Incarnate Son of God is through the cross and suffering to the splendour of the Resurrec-

tion.' To arrive with the Son of Man through suffering and
death at this splendour of Resurrection is the road for
each one of us for all peoples.[12]

The conflicts that engulfed Europe from 1939 onwards cast
a pall of darkness and suffering. Edith and her community
prayed the Divine Office while overhead the planes of the
Luftwaffe roared on their way to bomb Britain. She was ever
more conscious of the growing persecution of Jewish people
and after 1940, with the Netherlands under German rule, she
knew that the SS were ready to seek her out. She had the
comfort of her sister Rosa's presence, for Rosa, now a Roman
Catholic, had made her way to Echt and was serving the
Carmel as its extern sister.

In 1942 Sister Antonia, the new Prioress at Echt, asked
Edith to write a book on John of the Cross to commemorate
the fourth century of his birth. Edith was delighted with the
possibility as she had reflected on John's writings over the
years. She had few resources to write a critical study, but *The
Science of the Cross* is an attempt to grasp John's teaching
through insights into the unity of his person, his very being.
She tried to draw together in a whole his writings, his life and
his prayer. She was fascinated by John's drawing of Christ
Crucified, and saw the suffering Christ already radiating the
power of the Resurrection. Edith did not finish this study, nor
did she have the chance to revise what she had written.
However, she saw in John's writings much about the truth of
the Cross and the saving work Jesus achieved through his
death in loving obedience. She saw the dark night as the way
we can enter the Easter mystery and journey through apparent
failure and abandonment to the new, undreamt of life that is
Resurrection. She saw the Cross shining through the darkness
of being unloved and unrecognised. Edith realised that it was
the terrible way he was misunderstood that caused John to
suffer and know terrible darkness, even doubt, when imprisoned in Toledo. Again she saw the suffering caused by
misunderstanding and mean-spiritedness that marked his last

months as another aspect of living the Cross. At the time she wrote, the Nazis were beginning to harass her and the shadow of death was imminent. She now saw her suffering and John's as ways of living the Cross of Jesus. As a Carmelite Edith lived out and reproduced the humanity of Christ and above all his subjection to the powers of this world and the final walk to Calvary.

On 2 August 1942 Edith and Rosa were taken by the SS and began a journey that would end with their death in Auschwitz on 9 August 1942. As they left the convent Edith took her sister by the hand and said 'Come, Rosa. We are going for our people.' Edith died because she was Jewish. Her arrest was a retaliation for the Dutch bishops' attack on the anti-Semitism of the regime: Catholics of Jewish birth were to be killed. We must also remember that, besides Edith and Rosa, two other members of their family died in Auschwitz, their sister Frieda and their brother Paul.

Like Titus, Edith had been passionate for the truth that she had lived to the full, using her outstanding intellectual gifts. But more than that, she had come to experience the reality of God and also known times of desert and darkness. She was a modern woman, a person of warmth and yet private because of her longing for God. Titus died because he was seen as a dangerous subversive, an enemy of the regime. Edith died because she was Jewish, and this fact is important. She is a saint because I believe that she came to know and love God after she had moved beyond atheism and climbed the mountain of the Lord. She came to a union with God in Jesus Christ and lived the Carmelite way to the full. However, it is important that the recognition of Edith Stein as a saint should not be a stumbling block to the relationship between Christians and Jews. It is easy for Christians to see Christianity as a fulfilment of Judaism. For Jews this is not so. Christianity is a quite other way, and the Jews continue to live with the messianic expectation. Thus ceasing to live as a Jew and becoming a Christian cannot be seen by Jews as 'fulfilment'. Perhaps fitting words, that may help Christian–Jewish dialogue and allow Edith Stein to work for truth even after her death, can be found in an article written by her niece Suzanne Batzdorff:

> Understanding can never be achieved by glossing over or by one side trying to convince the other that it alone is in possession of the truth. Too much pain and suffering have occurred over the centuries because people have followed the motto 'Und willst Du nicht mein Bruder sein, So schlag ich Dir den Schadel ein' ('If you refuse to be my brother, I smash your brains in').
>
> How much better to listen to our brothers' cry, to strive for the empathy that my aunt wrote about in her doctoral dissertation, to search for ways to help each other, to see the common humanity and grant to others the right to follow the path of their choice by which they reach our common goals.
>
> Some time ago we commemorated the 50th anniversary of Kristallnacht, the Night of Broken Glass, Nov. 9–10, 1938. It was the opening of the violent phase of the Holocaust, the pogrom in which synagogues were destroyed and people were arrested and shipped to concentration camps by the thousands. We commemorate, we mourn, but we must stand together and vow to be more sensitive in the future to the cry of human beings, to refuse to join the howling mob, to heal and rescue rather than cast stones and firebrands, and to fight injustice wherever we may find it. That is a goal worth fighting for; that is a purpose to which we can all dedicate ourselves, regardless of race, colour or religion.
>
> So far, the church has not found any bona fide miracles attributable to Edith Stein. But if I may paraphrase Father Donovan, if the memory of Edith Stein can inspire us to such courage and such resolve, that may perhaps be miracle enough.[13]

Perhaps our hope can be that Edith Stein, within the Communion of Saints, will work to free Christians for ever from the evils of anti-Semitism and that Christian believers will never allow their brothers and sisters to suffer in such a way again.

9. SYMBOLS AND FOCUS – ELIJAH AND MARY

As we have seen, the prophet Elijah was an important figure for medieval Carmelites. Beginning with the *rubrica prima* of the 1281 Constitutions, a myth was woven by Carmelites that presented Elijah as the great exemplar of prayer and the monastic life. He became a type of founding figure for the Order but, more importantly, he stood out as a person of prayer who came into the presence of God and who, in drinking from the stream Cherith, experienced the goodness of God. Elijah as the one who travelled to the East and found intimacy with God in prayer became an inspiration down the centuries for Carmelite brothers and sisters alike.

However, in the twentieth century Elijah, like all the prophets, is seen as passionate for the truth and for the revelation that comes from God in Scripture and fully in Jesus Christ. In his own day Elijah had to face the tyranny of Ahab and the anger of Jezebel. He opposed the superstitions introduced by Jezebel and the poverty brought about by the monarch dabbling in power politics. In the twentieth century, we have seen how Titus Brandsma and Edith Stein were passionate for the same truth and how their closeness to God gave them insight into human dignity. Both Titus and Edith opposed racism, and in their commitment to truth they recognised the fallacy of oppressive ideologies.

As the twentieth century progressed, Carmelites have realised that Elijah, like all prophets, was a champion of the poor and oppressed. Oppression in our century has come about through dictatorships and Marxist-Leninist states. Marxist-Leninism sought to deny the transcendent, but was never able to crush the Spirit. Carmelites have stood out against totalitarianism in Eastern Europe. However, the greatest misery and oppression has come from poverty and military dictatorships worldwide that have flouted human dignity by denying human rights. To hear the cry of the poor has become an imperative for Christians in many areas of the world. To oppose poverty during the Cold War era was to leave oneself open to being called a Communist and liable to face state violence. The struggle for justice has been embraced by Carmelites along with many others in the Church, but even inside the Church there can be misunderstanding, and those working for justice have faced hostility from some quarters. As the one who cared for the widow and for the poor, Elijah has helped Carmelites to discover a solidarity with the poor and to find a contemporary expression of the Elijan tradition. However, alongside expressions of practical love, an awareness has grown that for people to come to their full dignity they need to know and love God. For Carmelites reflection on the Scriptures has always been a foundation for their way of life. Hence in recent decades the practice of *lectio divina* has grown, not just as individual reflection, but also as a way of enabling the people we serve to know the living God. Reading the Scriptures, then reflecting and making connections with the realities of life – this practice is a powerful way to evangelise, share spirituality and find strength when the Gospel is ignored by those with power.

Pondering, reflecting, helps to create a desert, a special place in our being. But this faithful listening also reminds us of Mary, whom all Carmelites call their Mother and Sister. The current Constitutions of the Order express this succinctly:

> Mary, overshadowed by the Spirit of God,
> is the Virgin of the new heart,
> who gave a human face to the word made flesh.
> She is the Virgin of wise and contemplative listening
> who kept and pondered in her heart
> the events and words of the Lord.

She is the faithful disciple of wisdom,
who sought Jesus – God's Wisdom–
and allowed herself to be formed and moulded by his
  Spirit,
so that in faith she might be conformed to his ways and
  choices.
Thus enlightened, Mary is presented to us
as one able to read 'the great wonders'
which God accomplished in her
for the salvation of the humble and of the poor.

Mary was not only the Mother of Our Lord;
she also became his perfect disciple, the woman of faith.
She followed Jesus, walking with the disciples,
sharing their demanding and wearisome journey
– a journey which required, above all, fraternal love
and mutual service.[1]

The early Carmelites wove Mary and Elijah together as they created the Carmelite myth and told the story of their origins. Mary was symbolised by the small cloud Elijah saw rising from the sea. This cloud was life-giving and God-bearing for sinful humanity. The early Carmelites, who had dedicated their church on Carmel to Mary, saw her as both Mother and Sister. John Baconthorpe, a fourteenth-century English friar, said 'God willed to establish the brothers on Mount Carmel for the praise of his mother.' However, the use of the title 'sister' was adopted to show that Mary was close to the friars and that they were all disciples. Just as Mary had brought Christ to a waiting world, her Carmelite brothers (and today her Carmelite sisters) through their total allegiance to Jesus Christ would bring him to their own world. A Flemish Carmelite writing in 1479 synthesised much of the thought and devotion of his medieval confrères in the following passage:

It remains to be seen how the Brothers are to show love, full honour and fraternal reverence to such a Sister, a most excellent Mother and Patron who is of such sublime power, gentle piety, bounteous liberality and wholesome fruitfulness. For from all peoples she chose the Carmelites to be a race that would be special to herself, and particularly took them under the shadow of her wings; as the Loved One adopted by the Brothers, she indeed prays at every moment for them, her people, whom she as it were holds to her breasts and instructs with divine milk. I omit the special cult and devotions which day and night they do not cease to offer to the most divine, all powerful Mother which they so dearly love, most reverently venerate, most devoutly praise, magnify to the highest degree, and admiringly extol. In their hearts and mouths, they rightly proclaim a more special place for her. At least those things must be fixed in mind which bind the Carmelite family to the benefits of the divine Mary; they must with others display her most efficacious patronage in the midst of her people. They are to recognise as of right that they must eternally give thanks, for they do not have of themselves the ability to refer benefits to those who bestow them. And since, on the evidence of Pope Gregory, each one carries some title of his or her work, so that it can be easily seen under whose direction it is done, in addition all Churches of a Carmelite community are built in honour of the most glorious Mary and are called by her reverend name. Hence joyfully the whole of Carmel proclaims:

I have chosen the abode of the Mother of Christ for a house, there may the holy Virgin come to the aid of her servants.[2]

One expression of Mary as patron of the Order is the scapular devotion. The origins of this devotion are obscure. Links are made with St Simon Stock and thirteenth-century England, but historians have never been able to reach a satisfactory conclusion. However, the devotion has flourished in the Church since the late Middle Ages and still has a positive meaning for many today.

The scapular represents the Carmelite habit in miniature

and the acceptance of it reminds the wearer of Mary, both her protection and her total openness to God. It is also a 'sacramental', a sacred sign that is intended to open us to a fuller relationship with Christ. The wearing of the scapular is a sign of the basic Christian commitment in baptism, and a reminder to deepen the baptismal relationship with Christ in prayer.

The scapular is part of the popular devotional tradition of the Church. Popular devotions, when properly grounded, can be openings into the transcendent by reminding us that we need God's help and are not self-sufficient. It is crucial that we value symbols. Society today is full of symbols and images, yet many Christians tend to down-play or lose contact with symbolism and in this way lose a valuable way of communication which can touch the imagination.

Many Carmelites today would say that the Order's basic intuition about Mary is her presence. There has always been a sense of Mary's closeness, whether through liturgical and devotional practices, or through the awareness that by her support she was one who protected the Order. This sense of protection was expressed symbolically by the scapular devotion. Again the title 'Sister' underlined a sense of warmth and closeness that valued Mary as a person rather than as a role.

The question arises, how can this tradition of devotion and sense of personal presence help the Carmelite family as it works for the Kingdom of God on the threshold of a new millennium? The questions that challenge us most are issues of human dignity, justice, the role of women and our treatment of creation. The Roman Catholic Church tries to see Mary in the midst of the community as the model of redemption. She is the one who is the faithful disciple eagerly co-operating and enabling the work of redemption. Perhaps Carmel's role is to give this intellectual, theological vision warmth and humanity.

A further question that must be asked of the Carmelite tradition regarding Mary is how can it help the role of women in the Church? Chris O'Donnell makes the following observation:

Our values of fraternity and sorority give us an approach to the difficult issues concerning the role of women in the Church. The modern feminist movement is unanimous in its protest against any domination of women by men, against that corruption of the male role which feminism calls patriarchy. The Order's search for a fraternity and sorority which emphasises basic equality, co-responsibility, can at once make us open to the legitimate criticism, indeed anger of women, and at the same time help to protect us from ourselves taking part in the unjust systems of domination. The Carmelite intuition of Mary as Sister, moreover, is one which seems to be very attractive to some women.

Feminist writing on Mary covers a very wide spectrum. On the one hand we have positive studies of the Virgin by men and women who are sensitive to feminist concerns. But at the extremes there is an angry feminism which sees Mary as having been deliberately used by a patriarchal Church to keep women passive and servile. Such writers are often negative also about Mary herself.

The profound insight of Hans Urs von Balthasar about the primarily Marian character of the Church is one that should echo with our tradition. As we have always seen Mary as the model for all Carmelites, so we can easily be at home with a presentation of ecclesiology mainly in terms of its Marian, rather than its Petrine or institutional dimensions.

A further area in contemporary mariology is a strong emphasis on Mary as a woman in Palestine. Against pictures of the Virgin which, in glorifying her, succeeded in removing her from real humanity, there is now a search to discover Mary in her womanhood and in her femininity. Paul VI gave an initial sketch of an anthropological approach to Mary in *Marialis cultus* article 37. It is an important innovation in magisterial teaching, but we should perhaps take its thrust and inspiration rather than regard it as a definitive picture. The way in which the

Carmelite tradition has considered Mary as Mother and Sister, as well as her ubiquitous presence should allow us to develop easily an attractive picture of Mary as a woman. The picture of the easy relationships between Mary and her Carmelite followers on Mount Carmel in the early legendary material gives a good basis for such reflection.[3]

Creative collaboration is beginning to emerge inside the Carmelite family between friars and women Carmelites. We must always remember that the creative re-imagining of Carmel in the sixteenth century was largely the work of Teresa and that the revitalising of the tradition is essential today.

The struggle for women's rights in the Church is one that must be on the agenda of the Carmelite family if it is to be faithful to its Marian and prophetic tradition. Men and women image God, and a church that for whatever reason excludes and seems to ignore half the human race would be failing in its redemptive mission.

Issues of justice in general are crucial if we are to be faithful to the call to enable God's Kingdom to come. Mary in her Magnificat is recognised as expressing such concerns. The Congregation for the Doctrine of Faith in its instruction 'On Christian Freedom and Liberation' says incisively that at the side of Christ, Mary 'is the most perfect image of freedom and of the liberation of humanity and of the universe'.

Carmelite mariology has much then to offer liberation theologies. Mary is not only the icon of liberation, but she is the one who as Mother and Sister draws us into a liberating struggle. But the teaching on the Pure Heart is a major protection against the deviations that anger, guilt, indeed self-seeking, can bring to the service of the poor. Mary as the Virgin Most Pure can teach us how to listen to, and learn from the poor, as well as being at their service. Indeed it is only with great purity of heart that it is safe to enter into the 'lucha' or struggle for freedom.[4]

Perhaps as we try to interlink modern approaches to Mary with a long tradition in the Carmelite Order of devotion to the Mother of God it would be good to include two texts, one old and one new, that help us to come to an understanding.

The first text, *Flos Carmeli*, goes back to the Middle Ages and celebrates the beauty of Mary. Beauty is not something cosmetic, but rather is a radical celebration of goodness, the goodness of God and all creation:

> Flower of Carmel,
> Blossoming vine,
> Splendour of heaven,
> Child-bearing Virgin,
> None like to thee.
> Mother so tender,
> Who no man did know,
> To Carmel's children,
> Be gracious,
> O star of the sea.[5]

While finally the Preface from the Mass in honour of Our Lady of Mount Carmel echoes Vatican II and celebrates traditional images:

> Father, all-powerful and ever-living God,
> we do well always and everywhere to give you thanks
> as we honour the Blessed Virgin Mary.
> She shares with Christ his work of salvation,
> and with his Church she brings forth sons and daughters
> whom she calls to walk the path of perfect love.
> She claims us also as her beloved children,
> clothed in the habit of her Order,
> shields us along our way of holiness,
> and in her likeness sets us before the world,
> so that our hearts, like hers,
> may ever contemplate your Word,
> love our brothers and sisters,

and draw them to her Son.
In our joy we sing to your glory
with all the choirs of angels.[6]

EPILOGUE – CARMELITE SPIRITUALITY AND THE POST-MODERN

Can the Carmelite tradition offer a spirituality of substance to the post-modern world? The world of 'the modern' with its individualism and materialism is over. While one reaction could be to become free-floating and superficial, there is also a yearning for a way that is creative and capable of healing the terrible wounds of the twentieth century. It is possible to detect a desire to live not as isolated and self-absorbed individuals, but as people able to go beyond the self and to reach out to ultimate values. A hope is emerging that we can build bridges between our daily experience and God.

Our culture, our way of life at the end of the twentieth century, is lived very much on the surface. We are surrounded by images and sound bites, and the relentless search for something new and sensational saps our energy. This way of life can take away wonder and any capacity for inner awareness. In this context so much that is genuinely human and life-enhancing can be lost to view. We risk ignoring the capacity of the heart to wonder, to search, to listen and to experience that deepest of emotions, compassion. We need to give our imagination freedom so that we can make connections and really see and hear what is going on around us. We all need to develop a poetic sense so that we can celebrate life and give our imaginations permission to flourish. This sense of freedom and openness helps us to know ourselves better and to realise that we are all called to be 'artists' who are engaged on the project of shaping the unique individual that each one of us is, to enable this individual to reach full potential and to give expression to the longing expressed by Augustine – 'our hearts

are restless until they rest in God'. However, as we discover
the beauty that is within and around us, we are not meant to
retreat into a narcissistic self-absorption, but rather to be
energised to reach out to a world full of hunger and needs.
Journeying into our heart we recognise inner riches and realise
that we cannot be satisfied with the current cultural orthodoxy.
There has to be more!

How does the Carmelite tradition speak to these needs and
help the awakening sensibilities of a post-modern world? Our
world needs a sense of community and a genuine hope that
the wounds of the world can be healed. Living on the surface,
in a culture of images and sound bites, we have lost touch with
the skill of listening. Listening, pondering, treasuring in the
heart are values that matter to Carmelites. The Rule asks that
Carmelites immerse themselves in the Scriptures. This form
of listening opens us to the presence of the mystery that is God,
that is unconditional love. A steady listening, attentiveness to
the mystery is what we mean by contemplation. The prerequi-
sites for such listening are solitude and silence. We need to
find a place and a time to stop and to be, rather than merely
to do. However, listening in silence and openness to the
mystery that is God is not meant to make us self-absorbed or
feel superior. The light that comes from listening gives us
energy to move away from egoism. We see what can be, or
have become, the false gods and idols in our lives. This freedom
from lesser gods is what is meant by purity of heart, which is
an important element in the Carmelite tradition. It means
that we desire to live in allegiance to Jesus Christ and to his
work which is the establishment of the Kingdom of God. A
pure heart means that, as we become aware of the free gift of
God's love, we will want to love others in a way that is truly
liberating, life-enhancing and respectful of human dignity. We
have received freely from God's generosity. Therefore we want
to respond to that love and to give thanks for it by helping
others enter the banquet of eternal life. As Gustavo Gutiérrez
said, 'Mystical language expresses the gratuitousness of God's

love, prophetic language expresses the demands this love makes whole.'[1]

However, for Carmelites, the imperative of prayer that asks us to love and serve others as God loves us finds its initial expression in community life. From the first days on Carmel, the brothers came out of their solitude to meet, to celebrate Eucharist and to grow in understanding together. In a society that is so often violent, fragmented and far from peace, the poetry of people who live together in a community of friendship is a potent sign. A real community of friendship is a healing reality for others and also an antidote to the scramble for power, wealth and money. In our own day, unbridled capitalism has become, as Pope John Paul II suggests, a new 'fascism' with currency speculators blighting economies and making the poor poorer. On a personal level consumerism as a way of life tears the heart out of our relationships. I *become* the Gucci, the car, the house and the holiday. However, where brothers and sisters share life in simplicity and love, hope may emerge. When Teresa of Avila renewed Carmel she saw the quality of human relationships as the key test. The ideal she proclaimed was 'All must be friends, all must be loved, all must be held dear, all must be helped.' If we are a community of friendship and simplicity our energy will be freed to work for justice.

> The Generals of the two Carmelite orders have urged such a witness for today's world: We are talking about community which is born out of listening to the Word of God, and so humanises its members, brings people together despite their differences and is thus a true presence of the Gospel. In this way our communities will become signs of hope which will cause the poor to say about us what the widow of Zarapeta said about Elijah, 'Now I know that you are truly a man of God and that the word of the Lord in your mouth is truth' (1 Kings 17:24).[2]

The Carmelite tradition today would say, therefore, that listening, recognising the wisdom of the heart, brings us to that contemplative state that opens us to God's loving pres-

ence. The tradition would also say that this contemplative
stance is not tied to a method, but rather depends on the
cultivation of time and a place for God and a willingness to
allow the word of God in Scripture to be the main source of
our nurture. This contemplative prayer, which opens us to the
gift of God's love, then draws us into solidarity with all who
are in need of God's mercy. In the first instance, the openness
to 'the other' is shown in the warmth of a community of friendship, but then we must move on to serve the people around us
with their many and varied needs. We are called to utter a
word of love that shows itself in acts of compassion. Our gratitude towards God is best shown in our sensitive love for others.
The love we receive from God is, as Thérèse of Lisieux said,
all free – 'It is all grace.' So our response must also have a
spontaneous generosity.

Two contemporary Carmelites, Kees Waaijman and John
Welch, have reflected on the closing lines of the Rule and have
something to say that may help us respond to today's needs.
The concluding lines of the Rule are as follows; 'Here then are
a few points I have written down to provide you with a standard of conduct to live up to: *but Our Lord at his Second
Coming will reward anyone who does more than he is obliged
to.'*

According to Welch and Waaijman this passage seems to
refer to the parable of the Good Samaritan. The Carmelite is
the Innkeeper and Christ has come bringing the sick and the
wounded asking that they be cared for – that everything possible be done to help. Christ will return and then repay the
Innkeeper. According to this interpretation the Carmelite has
his or her world turned upside down by the visit of Christ. We
are asked to care for people with all their needs and wounds.
This request, which causes inconvenience, challenges the Carmelite out of any egocentricity and reminds him or her that
life is a mess and unpredictable. Spirituality is not a cosy
option but is the call to respond to the gift of God's love by
our involvement in what is often a dark and difficult world.
Waaijman suggests: 'Real giving is essentially dark, and this

is 'the going beyond' of The Rule into a desert of love, a night of trust.' For many people today, life is grim and dark, and if we are to help we have to travel into that same darkness. I can think of my own tidy life being thrown into confusion when I agreed to help an asylum-seeker. The demands that flowed from helping were complex, whether it was a question of facing the Kafkaesque bureaucracy of the Immigration system or of learning of the torture and brutality that the man I helped had endured and still endures. In our British society, we are coming to realise more and more the extent of abuse, physical and sexual, that people suffered and still suffer.

In another context there is the harshness of the world of commerce that so often uses people, burns them up and leaves them broken and abandoned. This is not to mention those who struggle with addiction or live with addicts, or again those affected by AIDS who need support and are so often subject to prejudice even sometimes from fellow Christians. These are the dark places and these are the wounded people of our times. When we allow their needs to break into our lives we can respond to God's love by becoming love ourselves. This, perhaps, is the way that Carmel's contemplative tradition can become real in our own day and age.

I would like to conclude with two quotations. The first is from John Welch:

> The Presence whom Carmelites have been contemplating for almost eight hundred years is a night that guides, an absence that reveals, a flame that heals. The Carmelite tradition offers a language for the soul helping to disclose this Presence deep within our lives. It is a language, ultimately, of attentive stillness, awaiting the lover's approach. This Carmelite way, born of the attempt to live in allegiance to Jesus Christ, is an ancient path for today's pilgrim.[3]

Here I believe my American confrère has in a special poetry focused the vision of what Carmel is and wants to be.

Finally, I would like to offer Chapter VI of our Constitutions as an attempt to say how our tradition desires to live its contemplative prayer in practice:

Our Apostolic Mission – General Considerations

91. Our Carmelite mission shares in the mission of Jesus,

who was sent to proclaim the Good News of the Kingdom of God

and to bring about the total liberation of humanity from all sin and oppression.

Our ministry as Carmelites is, therefore, an integral part of our charism.

We are guided in this by the teaching of the pastors of the Church;

by our tradition

and by the values it upholds;

by the signs of the times;

and above all, by attentive listening to the Word,

having regard also for its interpretation

from the perspective of the poor.

We are to evaluate and renew our service (*diakonia*) in the church,

so that we may better respond to the questions raised

by the cultural, social and religious circumstances of the people.

In our mission, we must take into account

the talents and charisms of the brethren,

and be aware of the natural limitations of our contribution.

92. We Carmelites must fulfil our mission among the people

first and foremost through the richness of our contemplative life.

Our prophetic action may take many and different forms of apostolic service.

Since not all forms of apostolic work easily fit in with our charism

or with the resources of our individual community,
we must always discern among the various options
   presented in any given situation.

93. Inspired by the fundamental directions of our
   charism
and by the present-day ecclesial and social contexts,
the following guidelines are offered
for the discernment of our apostolic mission:
  – a life of brotherhood and prayer in the midst of the
    people;
  – a response to the needs of the local and universal
    Church;
  – a preferential service to the poor and the
    marginalized;
  – a special attention to issues concerning women;
  – a commitment to justice and peace;
  – a care for those who show an interest in the spirit,
    the spiritual heritage, and the life of Carmel.
In these ways we commit ourselves to listening to God,
as he speaks to us in Scripture and in the history of
   our people.

94 We shall therefore study needs and demands,
both religious and social, in every time and place
so that we may strengthen our witness
to a spirit of community among all the People of God,
by means of various appropriate apostolic activities,
initiated and implemented in a spirit of fraternal
   co-operation.

95. Faithful to the spiritual heritage of the Order,
we shall therefore channel our diverse works
to the goal of promoting the search for God
and the life of prayer.
In our various apostolates we shall be inspired by Mary:
her presence among the Apostles;
her motherhood in the Church,

which she received at the foot of the Cross;
her attentiveness to the Word of God,
and her total obedience to the divine will.
To this end, we shall foster and nourish among the people
the memory of Mary and devotion to her.

96. In the Scriptures and in Carmelite tradition,
the prophet Elijah is respected as the one
who in various ways knew how to read the new signs
of the presence of God
and who was able, not least,
to reconcile those who had become strangers or enemies.

As Carmelites, heartened by this example
and by our strong desire to put into practice our Lord's
    teachings
of love and reconciliation,
we shall take part in the ecumenical movement
and in inter-religious dialogue,
promoted by the Second Vatican Council.
Through the former we shall promote relationships
with the Orthodox and other Christians.
Through the latter we shall promote dialogue at various
    levels
with Jews and Muslims,
with whom we share devotion to the prophet Elijah as a
    man of God;
we shall enter into dialogue also with Hindus and
    Buddhists
and those of other religions.

Moreover, Carmelites are to make themselves available
to accompany those who genuinely desire
to experience the transcendent in their lives
or who wish to share their experience of God.[4]

NOTES

INTRODUCTION

1. *Journey with Carmel* (Carmelite Publications, Middle Park, Victoria, Australia, 1977), p. 73.

CHAPTER 1: THE FIRST HERMITS – A WAY OF LIFE

1. Joachim Smet O. Carm, *The Carmelites*, Vol. 1 (Carmelite Spiritual Center, Illinois, 1988), p. 3.
2. Hugh Clarke and Bede Edwards (eds.), *The Rule of St Albert* (Aylesford and Kensington, 1973).
3. *Carmelus* 441 (1997), p. 47.

CHAPTER 2: CHANGE AND TENSION

1. John Welch O. Carm, *The Carmelite Way* (Gracewing, 1996), p. 13.
2. Nicholas the Frenchman, *The Flaming Arrow*, trans. Bede Edwards in *The Sword* (June 1979), p. 23.
3. *The Flaming Arrow*, p. 36.
4. *The Flaming Arrow*, p. 42. 'Stepsons' are those who in his view are not genuine Carmelites.

CHAPTER 3: ELIJAH AND MARY – SEARCH FOR IDENTITY

1. Adrian Staring, *Medieval Carmelite Heritage* (Carmelite Institute, Rome, 1989), p. 40.
2. Paul Chandler O. Carm (ed.), *A Journey with Elijah* (Carmelite Institute, Rome, 1991), p. 14.
3. *A Journey with Elijah*, p. 112.
4. *Liber de Institutione Primorum Monachorum*, draft trans. Paul Chandler O. Carm.

5. 'Choruses from "The Rock"' in T. S. Eliot, *Collected Poems 1909–62* (Faber, London, 1963).
6. *Medieval Carmelite Heritage*, p. 40.
7. Chris O'Donnell O. Carm, 'Mary and the Carmelite Tradition' (unpublished article), pp. 18–19.

CHAPTER 5: THE MYSTIC WAY

1. *Interior Castle* in *Collected Works of St Teresa of Avila*, vol. 2, trans. Kieran Kavanaugh OCD and Otilio Rodriguez OCD (Washington Province of Discalced Carmelites, ICS Publications, 2131 Lincoln Road N.E., Washington DC 20002, © 1980).
2. *The Life: Autobiography* in *Collected Works of St Teresa of Avila*, vol. 1, trans. Kieran Kavanaugh OCD and Otilio Rodriguez OCD (Washington Province of Discalced Carmelites, ICS Publications, 2131 Lincoln Road N.E., Washington DC 20002, © 1976).
3. *Regesta John Baptist Rossi*, ed. B. Zimmerman OCD (Rome, 1936), pp. 88–9.
4. *Book of Foundations* in *Collected Works of St Teresa of Avila*, vol. 3, trans. Kieran Kavanaugh OCD and Otilio Rodriguez OCD (Washington Province of Discalced Carmelites, ICS Publications, 2131 Lincoln Road N.E., Washington DC 20002, © 1985).
5. *Dark Night* in *Collected Works of St John of the Cross*, trans. Kieran Kavanaugh OCD and Otilio Rodriguez OCD (Washington Province of Discalced Carmelites, ICS Publications, 2131 Lincoln Road N.E., Washington DC 20002, © 1979, 1991).

CHAPTER 6: OVERWHELMED BY GOD'S LOVING PRESENCE – JOHN OF ST SAMSON AND LAWRENCE OF THE RESURRECTION

1. *L'Aiguillon* in *Complete Works of John of St Samson*, ed. Hein Blommestijn O. Carm and Max Huot de Longchamp (1992), p. 85.
2. *Brother Lawrence of the Resurrection: On the Practice of the Presence of God*, trans. Salvatore Scuirba (Washington Province of Discalced Carmelites, ICS Publications, 2131 Lincoln Road N.E., Washington DC 20002, © 1994), p. 52.
3. *On the Practice of the Presence of God*, pp. 39–43.

CHAPTER 7: LOVE IN THE HEART OF THE CHURCH – THÉRÈSE OF LISIEUX

1. *St Thérèse of Lisieux: Her Last Conversations*, trans. John Clarke (Washington Province of Discalced Carmelites, Inc., ICS Publications, 2131 Lincoln Road N.E., Washington DC 20002, © 1977), Aug/258.
2. *Thérèse of Lisieux: Story of a Soul*, trans. John Clarke (Washington Province of Discalced Carmelites Friars, Inc., ICS Publications, 2131 Lincoln Road N.E., Washington DC 20002, © 1975, 1976), p. 194.
3. *The Poetry of St Thérèse of Lisieux*, trans. Donald Kinney (Washington Province of Discalced Carmelites, Inc., ICS Publications, 2131 Lincoln Road N.E., Washington DC 20002, © 1995), pp. 153–4.

CHAPTER 8: TRUTH AND PROPHECY – EDITH STEIN AND TITUS BRANDSMA

1. Titus Brandsma O. Carm, *Carmelite Mysticism – Historical Sketches* (Carmelite Press, Illinois, 1996), p. 15.
2. *Essays on Titus Brandsma*, ed. Redemptus Valabek O. Carm (Carmel in the World Paperbacks, Rome, 1985), p. 284.
3. *Essays on Titus Brandsma*, p. 295.
4. *Carmelite Mysticism – Historical Sketches*, p. 111.
5. Waltraud Herbstrith, *Edith Stein: A Biography* (Harper & Row, San Francisco, 1985), p. 15.
6. *Edith Stein: A Biography*, p. 29.
7. *Edith Stein: A Biography*, p. 29.
8. Edith Stein, *Woman* in *Collected Works*, vol. 2, trans. Freda Mary Oben (Institute of Carmelite Studies, Washington DC, 1987), p. 145.
9. *Edith Stein: A Biography*, p. 89.
10. *Edith Stein: Selected Writings*, ed. Suzanne M. Batzdorff (Templegate, Springfield IL, 1990), p. 93.
11. Edith Stein, *Mystery of Christmas* (Darlington Carmel, 1998), p. 15.
12. *Mystery of Christmas*, p. 16.
13. *Edith Stein: Selected Writings*, p. 118.

CHAPTER 9: SYMBOLS AND FOCUS – ELIJAH AND MARY

1. *Carmelite Constitutions* (Carmelite Publications, Middle Park, Victoria, Australia, 1996), p. 20.
2. Chris O'Donnell O. Carm, 'Mary and the Carmelite Tradition' (unpublished article), p. 27. (This excerpt from *De Patronatu* by

Arnoldus Bostius shows great warmth and expresses a devotion that flows from deep love and prayer and praise in the liturgy.)
3. 'Mary and the Carmelite Tradition', p. 76.
4. 'Mary and the Carmelite Tradition', p. 77.
5. Anonymous English translation.
6. Preface from *The Carmelite Missal* (Rome, 1979).

EPILOGUE: CARMELITE SPIRITUALITY AND THE POST-MODERN

1. Gustavo Gutiérrez, *Job* (Claretian Publications, 1987), p. 95.
2. John Welch O. Carm, *The Carmelite Way* (Gracewing, 1996), p. 153.
3. *The Carmelite Way*, p. 174.
4. *Carmelite Constitutions* (Carmelite Publications, Middle Park, Victoria, Australia, 1996), pp. 49–51.

BIBLIOGRAPHY

Chandler, Paul, O. Carm (ed.), *A Journey with Elijah* (Rome: Casa Editrice Institutum Carmelitanum, 1991).

Cicconetti, Carlo, O. Carm, *The Rule of Carmel*, trans. Gabriel Pausback O. Carm, ed. Paul Hoban O. Carm (Darien IL: Carmelite Spiritual Center, 1984).

Herbsrith, Waltraud, *Edith Stein* (San Francisco: Harper & Row, 1985).

The Collected Works of St John of the Cross, trans. Kieran Kavanaugh OCD and Otilio Rodriguez OCD (Washington DC: ICS Publications, 1991).

The Collected Works of St Teresa of Avila, 3 volumes, trans. Kieran Kavanaugh OCD and Otilio Rodriguez OCD (Washington DC: ICS Publications, 1976–1985).

Lawrence of the Resurrection, Br, *On the Practice of the Presence of God*, trans. Salvatore Scuirba OCD (Washington DC: ICS Publications, 1994).

Mulhall, Michael, O. Carm (ed.), *Albert's Way* (Rome: Institutum Carmelitanum, 1989).

O'Donnell, Chris, O. Carm, *Love in the Heart of the Church* (Dublin: Veritas, 1997).

Slattery, Peter, *The Springs of Carmel* (New York: Alba House, 1991).

Smet, Joachim, O. Carm, *The Carmelites*, 4 volumes (Darien IL: Carmelite Spiritual Center, 1976–1988).

Staring, Adrian, O. Carm (ed.), *Medieval Carmelite Heritage* (Rome: Institutum Carmelitanum, 1989).

Thérèse of Lisieux, St, *Story of a Soul*, trans. and ed. John Clarke OCD (Washington DC: ICS Publications, 1975).

Valabek, Redemptus (ed.), *Titus Brandsma: Carmelite, Educator, Journalist, Martyr* (Rome: Carmel in the World Paperbacks, 1985).

Welch, John, O. Carm, *The Carmelite Way* (Leominster: Gracewing Fowler Wright, 1996).

Williams, Rowan, *Teresa of Avila* (Harrisburg PA: Morehouse Publishing, 1991).